DESTINATION UNKNOWN

Adventures of a World War II American Red Cross Girl

By
LeOna Kriesel Cox and Kathleen Cox

Dear Ileene —
Get better
soon! Time to
play again.
All best,
Kathie

"I met LeOna Kriesel Cox on an airplane. She told me about her World War II experiences. Although I met her only once, when I read the book **she came alive to me**; she was continuing to tell me story after story and again, I listened in awe. Then I realized I was not on the airplane listening to LeOna, rather I was reading the book so wonderfully put together by her daughter."

Nalini Juthani, M.D.
Scarsdale, New York

"**I was so drawn into these letters** from the very beginning and especially captivated by the stories about LeOna striking a bargain with Pope Pius XII, and keeping a crazed GI from taking the life of a Yugoslavian medic. She was an amazing woman.

As an educator I'm thrilled that LeOna's experiences can be shared with another generation. The important role of Red Cross girls in WWII can not be forgotten.

I highly recommend this book."

Betsy Smetana
Springfield, Virginia

"LeOna Kriesels' stories as told through her letters home are **poignant, yet upbeat**. Poignant for what is obliquely said about the soldiers' real lives in war. Upbeat, because she is young with personality and resilience to make a difference, one soldier at a time. And she tells how she did, on behalf of so many Red Cross girls like her, for our "boys" in uniform away from home."

Suzann Parker Leist
Crittenden, Kentucky

We've heard the greatest generation's battlefield stories many times. Now we have a chance to **hear the rest of the story** through a series of astonishing letters from a young Midwestern woman who joined the Red Cross to do her part in World War II.

Although in an epic context, this is a compelling personal narrative that remains focused on individual stories and concerns and concludes with a story book ending that even a more jaded generation will appreciate. **I felt like a fellow adventurer.**

Dr. David Kohl
Dean and University Librarian
Emeritus/University of Cincinnati
Senior Fulbright Scholar

You've never glimpsed WWII from this perspective before! This firsthand account by a small town American woman who bravely joined the war effort is a marvel of courage, adventure, delight and wonder.

Her stories conveyed through her letters home are lovingly compiled by her daughter in this wonderful book. It will make you laugh, cry and marvel at the spirit of this woman who in the 1940's couldn't have imagined what was in store for her as she boarded a troop ship for parts unknown.

Linda Kammire Tiffan, Ph.D.
Sarasota, Florida

ISBN 978-1466412484

Dedication

For Mindi and Bear

Acknowledgements

So many people helped and supported me through the four-year process of writing this book. I would like to sincerely thank each and every one of them.

They include my adult children and their spouses, Mindi (Markatos) and Tom MacKinnon, Eileen and Spencer (Bear) Markatos. They were cheerleaders all the way.

Christie and George Hamilton, dear friends for over 40 years; George, United States Military Academy 1963, an avowed history buff, provided invaluable help with military and World War II history and understanding.

Lucille Pederson Hardgrove Ph.D, a close family friend, spent over a year researching Red Cross and World War II history and guiding my progress.

David F. Kohl, Editor-in-Chief, Journal of Academic Librarianship, for his invaluable editorial review and professional support.

Angela Rinaldi, Barbara Baxter, Bob Wright, Carolyn (Pete) Wanner, Carolyn Caldwell, Carolyn Wall, Kay Wilber, Marcia Corey, Melinda Meickle, Nonie Johnson, Sue Anderson and Tom Wanner have offered helping hands, advice and support. I am grateful to all of them and others too numerous to name.

Finally, to Marti McGinnis, my artistic director and marketing genius who pulled it all together with her characteristic flair. Thank you Marti.

Kathleen Cox
2011

TABLE OF CONTENTS

"The Red Cross, with its clubs for recreation, its coffee and doughnuts in the forward areas, its readiness to meet the needs of the well and to help minister to the wounded has often seemed the friendly hand of this nation, reaching across the sea to sustain its fighting men."

**General Dwight D. Eisenhower
Address to Congress, June 18, 1945**

I'M ON MY WAY!

Onboard
Empress of Scotland
November 1943

Dear Mom and Dad,
I'm on my way! It's all
so exciting I just have
to tell you everything.
As we sailed from port
a military band played
on shore. Everyone hung
from the railings and
sang along with the band.
When the band struck up
"Over There, Over There,"
people really got ex-
cited. We can't wait to
get where we're going
and find out where it is!
We're on the most beauti-
ful ship you could ever
imagine.

So began one of over 200 letters written to family and friends back home. The writer was a 27-year-old Red Cross girl from Ortonville, Minnesota. Her name was LeOna Kriesel. LeOna had recently completed training in Washington, D.C. and nearby Virginia; now it was time to go to work. LeOna wrote this letter as she sailed aboard the luxurious Empress of Scotland, a ship that once epitomized the golden age of luxury sea travel. Now she served as a World War II troop carrier.

1943

LeOna Kriesel

Wartime security precautions did not permit anyone but the captain to know the ship's final destination. Most of the passengers were soldiers heading into battle; the others were nurses and Red Cross girls. What lay ahead was as mysterious as their "Destination Unknown."

13

Print the complete address in plain block letters in the panel below, and your return address in the space provided. Use typewriter, dark ink, or pencil. Write plainly. Very small writing is not suitable.

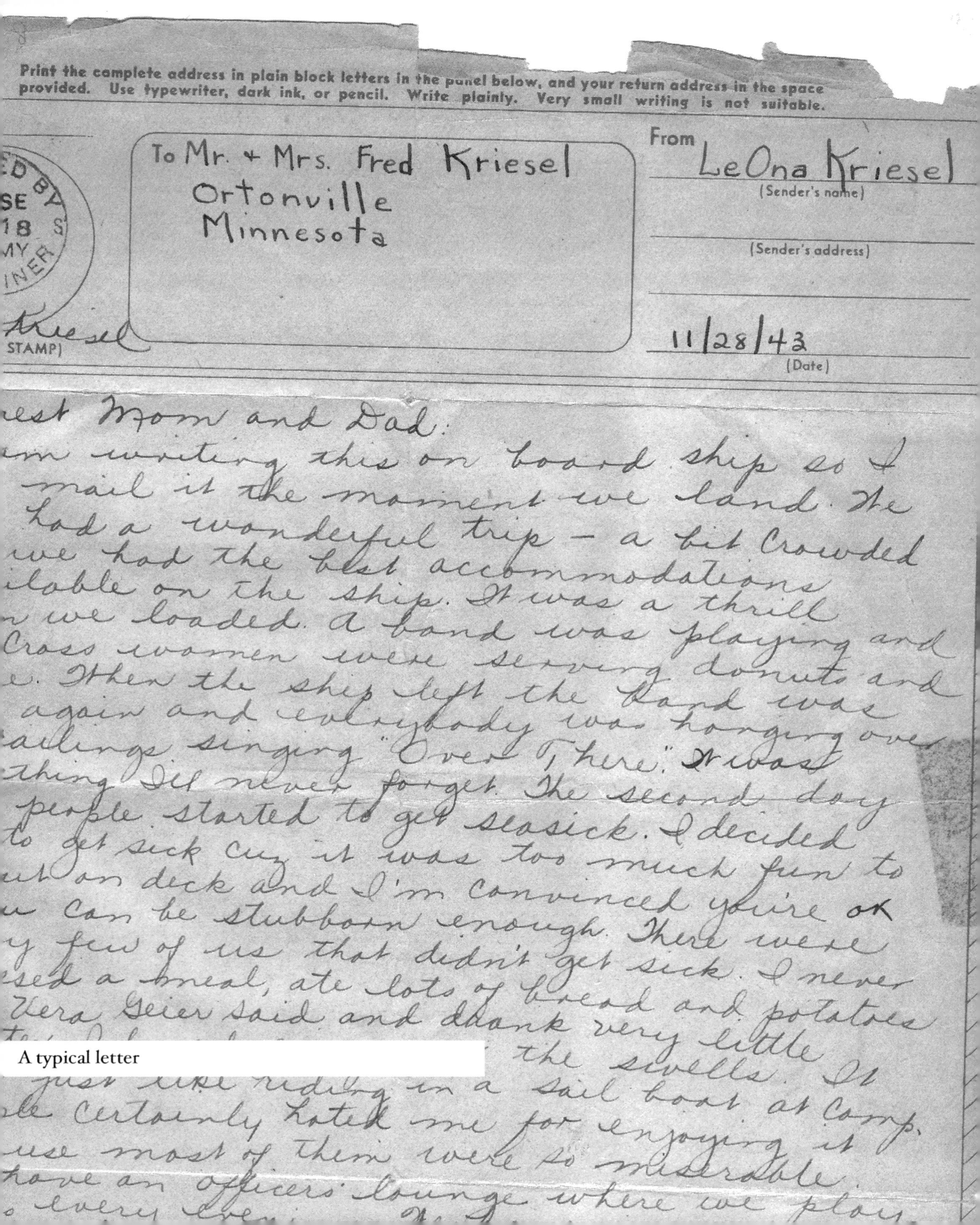

To Mr. & Mrs. Fred Kriesel
Ortonville
Minnesota

From LeOna Kriesel
(Sender's name)

(Sender's address)

11/28/43
(Date)

ED BY
SE
18 S
MY
INER
riesel
STAMP)

est Mom and Dad:
m writing this on board ship so I
mail it the moment we land. We
had a wonderful trip — a bit crowded
we had the best accommodations
ilable on the ship. It was a thrill
n we loaded. A band was playing and
Cross women were serving donuts and
e. When the ship left the band was
again and everybody was hanging over
ailings singing "Over There." It was
thing I'll never forget. The second day
people started to get seasick. I decided
to get sick cuz it was too much fun to
ut on deck and I'm convinced you're OK
u can be stubborn enough. There were
y few of us that didn't get sick. I never
sed a meal, ate lots of bread and potatoes
Vera Geier said and drank very little
the swells. It
just like riding in a sail boat at Camp.
le certainly hated me for enjoying it
use most of them were so miserable.
have an officers' lounge where we play
every eve

A typical letter

There are a combination of soldiers, nurses and American Red Cross
girls on board, 1,300 soldiers and 400 women. The second day out
people started getting seasick but not me. I made up my mind I
wasn't going to get sick because I was having too much fun. You
know me I believe you can do anything if you're stubborn enough. I
haven't missed a meal and I love going over the swells, it reminds
me of being in a sailboat when I worked at camp. People hate me for
enjoying myself when most of them are so miserable.

At night we play cards in the officer's club or we dance. Several soldiers are professional musicians who played with Gene Krupa,
Woody Herman and Harry James before they were drafted. The music is
wonderful and the soldiers love to dance.

There's been a little excitement along the way. We aren't travel-
ing in a convoy and twice there have been unidentified submarine
alerts. The first time we were asleep in our bunks when orders
came to stay put and hold on tight. The ship began zig-zagging
wildly as we hung on for dear life. It was all we could do not to
fall out of bed. That zig-zagging was to keep the submarine from
getting a fix on our exact location. Thankfully it was an American
sub.

We had another alert a few nights later but that time we were or-
dered to come up on deck and put on life vests. We were cautioned
to stand by the lifeboats and remain perfectly still. We weren't
to make a sound, or move, or light a match. We all just stood in
the dark and waited. Once again we were lucky and the sub was one
of ours. As we stood there in the dark all I could think about
were Dad's parting words, "If you don't go near the water, you
don't get wet."

Don't worry about me though; I'm having the time of my life.

THE STORY

Above: LeOna and Emmett Kriesel
University of Minnesota graduation

What follows is a story unlike most told about World War II. This is a story of happiness told through the letters of a woman with indomitable spirit; a woman who always saw the bright side of things. She was my mother.

LeOna Kriesel became LeOna Kriesel Cox in Rome, Italy. In Constantine she had met and fallen in love with a dashing Army Air Corps officer from Boston, Lieutenant John Cox, whom she often refers to as "Johnny" in her letters. They married in Rome near the end of the war and spent the next 51 years together. I am their only child.

Growing up I listened to my mother tell these stories over and over again. She never tired of them but I confess I did. A few years ago, in a box of her belongings, I found a scrapbook. Inside were letters my grandmother Kriesel had saved, each neatly written on onionskin paper or V-mail. With them were photographs of a smiling young woman whose story I now share.

In 1943, LeOna Kriesel was a 27-year-old teacher of business studies at Allegheny College in Meadville, Pennsylvania. She graduated from the University of Minnesota in 1938, and worked as a secretary at the Dayton Company in Minneapolis before landing the job at Allegheny.

It was at Allegheny that LeOna befriended fellow teacher Chuck Irvin and his wife Louise. The three often enjoyed evenings together in the Irvin's home.

One night at dinner Chuck shared something about himself that came as quite a surprise to LeOna. He said that along with his teaching job he was a recruiter for the American Red Cross. He explained that his job was to identify and recruit capable young women to go overseas and help America win the war. To her further surprise Chuck said, "LeOna, I've been observing you and I think you have what it takes to be a Red Cross girl. Would you be interested?"

Without a moment's hesitation LeOna re-

19

Chuck and Louise Irvin

sponded, "Would I? You bet I would!"

With characteristic enthusiasm she threw herself into the three-step application process that began with Red Cross officials in Washington, D.C. If she met with their approval she would interview with FBI agents. If they approved she would then undergo a thorough background investigation. Only if she passed all three screenings would she be offered a position.

When LeOna left Washington to return to Allegheny she knew she had passed two of the three. Once back in Meadville it seemed forever before the coveted letter arrived from the Red Cross confirming she had passed the background investigation and welcoming her to service. She was given a report date to arrive at American University and told to pack a footlocker with everything she would need for at least two years. LeOna had never been so excited. She immediately tendered her resignation to Allegheny and called her parents to share the good news.

Hearing this as they sat in their warm Minnesota kitchen, having just finished dinner, Nettie and Fred did not share their daughter's enthusiasm. She was saying that she intended to leave a good job and go to war; incomprehensible to parents who lost all but $13.00 when the Ortonville bank closed. When that happened LeOna and her brother Emmett were students at the University of Minnesota in Minneapolis. Emmett was a

year older than LeOna but she had skipped a grade which allowed the siblings to enter university in the same freshman class. When the family lost their savings everyone pulled together, worked hard and pinched pennies to keep LeOna and Emmet in school.

Graduation day was one of great pride and celebration for the Kriesel family. LeOna graduated with degrees in business and education; Emmett was an engineer. Both had good jobs waiting.

When Emmett's bout with childhood tuberculosis disqualified him from military service, Nettie and Fred thought their worries were over. Never for a moment had it occurred to them LeOna would be the one to go. Reluctantly they gave her their support; the Kreisel children had been raised to honor their country, share their blessings and help those in need. Which was exactly what LeOna planned to do.

TRAINING
"THRILLED TO DEATH WITH EVERYTHING"

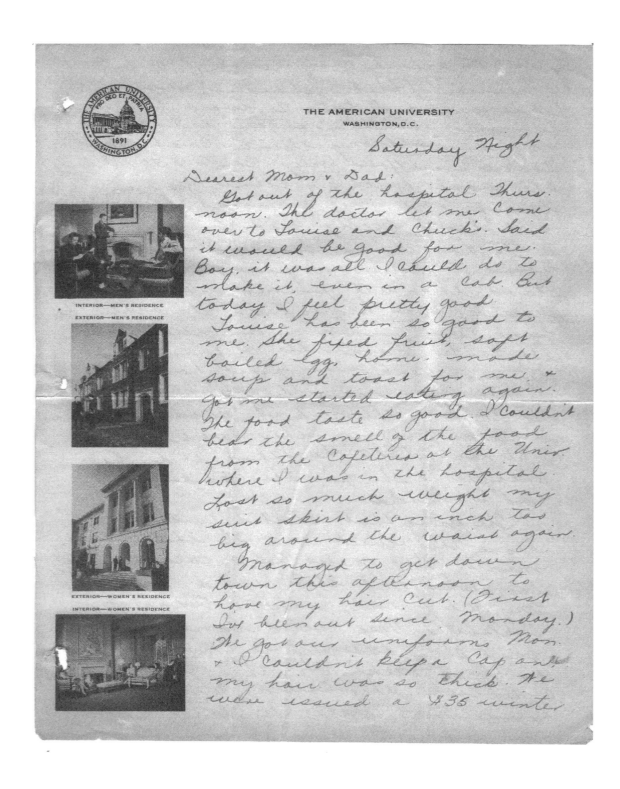

THE AMERICAN UNIVERSITY
WASHINGTON, D.C.

Saturday Night

Dearest Mom & Dad:

Got out of the hospital Thurs. noon. The doctor let me come over to Louise and Chuck's. Said it would be good for me. Boy, it was all I could do to make it, even in a cab. But today I feel pretty good

Louise has been so good to me. She fixed fried, soft boiled egg, home-made soup and toast for me, & got me started eating again. The food taste so good. I couldn't bear the smell of the food from the cafeteria at the Univ. where I was in the hospital. Lost so much weight my suit skirt is an inch too big around the waist again.

Managed to get down town this afternoon to have my hair cut. (First I've been out since Monday.) We got our uniforms Mom + I couldn't keep a cap on my hair was so thick. We were issued a $35 winter

INTERIOR—MEN'S RESIDENCE

EXTERIOR—MEN'S RESIDENCE

EXTERIOR—WOMEN'S RESIDENCE

INTERIOR—WOMEN'S RESIDENCE

Washington, D.C.
August 23, 1943

Dear Mom and Dad,
Training began today and I'm thrilled to death with everything. We registered all morning and have lectures this afternoon. The girls seem so nice; I've already met people from Texas, Oklahoma, California, Massachusetts, Ohio and Missouri. Even ran into one of my physical education teachers from university.

The Red Cross made nametags in the shape of our home states; we'll wear them until everyone gets acquainted. I met a swell girl from Boston in the train depot. She worked on the Boston Herald for eight years. Guess what, when we got our room assignments it turned out we're to be roommates.

We're living in a dormitory at American University. Unfortunately the girl at the train depot sent my luggage downtown to the New Colonial Hotel instead of American University. So while everyone else is all dolled up I'm sitting in the stinky old clothes I've had on since Wednesday.

Time to run for class so 'bye for now, it's plenty hot here in Washington!

Washington, D.C.
September 1943

Dear Mom & Dad,
Got mail today, first I've had. Almost finished with the first week of training and am thrilled to death with everything. I don't know when I've been so excited about a job. Seriously, the lectures we've been having are almost like fiction. I'm beginning to get a picture of what this war is really like. It's hard to know where to start there's so much to tell you.

First we had lectures on embarkation. Thought I'd tell you about that now as I won't be allowed to say anything once we go overseas. They made it very clear we had to keep our mouths shut! After the stuff they told us today I'm almost scared to write this much. Our instructor cited an example of a Red Cross girl who telephoned her parents in Montana and said she was in Colorado on her way to San Francisco. Well, her mother told the butcher, who told someone else and within three hours from the time she hung up the FBI called the Red Cross and reported what she had done. An entire convoy was held up because of it. So I'll tell you as much as I can now.

When we begin embarkation we'll be expected to carry our suitcases and march right along with the army. The instructor said to take light suitcases because we'll have to march about a mile. After hearing about a group of girls who had big suitcases like mine I decided to buy a new one. When the girls with the big suitcases got to the ship they found out they had to climb three inclines to get on deck, the last was really steep. Well the girls carried their suitcases up the first two inclines okay but when they got to the third they were so tired they started pushing the bags. As they gave their suitcases one good shove after another about 1,000 soldiers hung over the rails and yelled, "Heave, Ho!" The soldiers kept it up until one girl threw a regular tantrum; she was so exhausted she just stomped her feet and cried. Hearing that I decided a new suitcase was definitely in order.

We'll get training on the use of gas masks and go through a real gas chamber. Had a lecture on health today; we'll get a shot for small-pox, three for typhoid and three more for tetanus. Anyone going to the tropics will get additional shots for yellow fever, cholera and typhus. Those who find themselves in Africa and India will have to boil the milk and peel the fruit. The man in charge of clubs in China, Burma and India talked to us about snake charmers on the streets of India and about their caste system. He said Indian people will do our laundry but cautioned they beat clothes on rocks so they don't last very long. He also said to be careful of the monkeys and other wild animals. He mentioned one Red Cross girl who, when she went to the latrine in India, found a tiger on the roof and bees in the hole! I hope I'm not going to India.

Tonight we're going to a party at the Embassy Club. I'm having the time of my life; the girls I've met are tops. One worked for Mademoiselle magazine, another owned and ran a resort hotel in Mexico. Another girl taught in Paris for several years, we're going to take French lessons from her. One girl lived in China; one owned a private school in New York and Ralph Bellamy's son was one of her students. Told you, didn't I, my roommate was the society editor of the Boston Herald? Her name is Bettina Wilson.

There are also Red Cross men here and they have interesting stories too. One was in charge of recreation for all schools in Hawaii; another was a newspaperman with the Cincinnati Enquirer. Two others include a football coach from New York University in Albany and an FBI agent. Gotta quit now and get ready for the party.

Washington, D.C.
September 1943

Dear Mom and Dad,
Our second week of training is even more exciting than the first and I just love it. Monday we learned to play gin rummy, black jack, badminton, ping pong and several other card and dice games. Today we square danced all morning and learned how to call the dances; they say square dancing is one of the most popular forms of entertainment overseas. We got a sheet of cute calls so we can make it more fun. Boy, I'll really know how to put on a party once this war is over!

ALMOST TIME TO GO

Sandston, Virginia
October 1943

Dear Mom and Dad,
I'm in Sandston, Virginia now; we're working in a USO club to learn what we'll be doing overseas. It's a big club that serves 12,000 soldiers from the Army Air Corps base nearby.

Tuesday night I worked in a soda fountain. Someone asked for a cherry phosphate and in a panic I confessed my lack of experience. He said he didn't care so I told him if he'd drink whatever I mixed up it would be free. He drank the cherry phosphate down, grinned and didn't make any comment. I said, "Yes I know, it isn't like your mother used to make. Now let me whip up a grape for practice and that'll be free too." He swallowed the second one down. All evening he'd run up to me saying, "Look Miss, I'm not sick yet."

Then a little curly-haired kid, about 19, came up to me, smiled and said, "What do they call you? They call me Dave." Well, Dave had a jeep parked right out in front of the USO. When I told him how much I loved jeeps he took me for a ride. Think he tried to show off a bit because we fairly flew around the corners. I hung on with my knees and elbows and managed not to fall out.

The first night here some sergeant asked where I was from. When I said Minnesota he said most of his boys were from Minnesota. So Wednesday night the soda fountain was besieged with Minnesota boys from St. Cloud, Minneapolis, Windom, Amboy, Sisseton and Watertown. Everyone talked at once; they'd all been fishing in Big Stone Lake. They were so thrilled to see a girl from home. Most of them are kids right out of high school.

By Thursday night word must've gotten around the anti-aircraft unit that a Minnesota girl was at the USO because dozens of Iowa boys came down. Wanted to know if I knew anybody in Des Moines, Red Oak and all the other towns in Iowa that are close to Minnesota. Well

Sandston, Va.
Sept. 14, 1943

Dearest Mom & Dad:

I am now at the USO in Sandston. It's a swell place & it looks like fun. The building is new. Hard wood floors that are waxed & polished. The furniture is like in the golf club house at home. There is one very large room, very well furnished, a writing room with cute maple desks & chairs, books, magazines, newspapers etc. In the large room there is a snack bar with soda fountain. He run the fountain. There is a room with showers for the boys, too. The town itself is quite small but it

of course I did because when I worked at that camp on Lake Hubert we had campers from Iowa. One kid said he's going to Des Moines next week and he'd certainly have to tell his mother about meeting me.

Sandston, Virginia
October 1943

Dear Mom and Dad,
I've been dating a private first class here in Sandston. His name
is Riedemann and he comes from Iowa. Someone told his captain there
was a girl from the University of Minnesota at the USO so the captain came to see who it was. It turned out he's a boy I had classes
with in business school. The next day the captain called and asked
me to dinner. The call had to go through the switchboard and it
just so happened the operator was a friend of Riedemann's. The minute the GI put the captain's call through he called the signal department and reported the captain was calling Riedemann's girl.
Then he patched the signal corps in to listen to our conversation.

The guys in the signal corps took notes and when we hung up they
called down to the gun positions in the woods and read the tran-
script of our conversation. Riedemann was at one of the gun posts
and everyone started to razz him. Even the guys on guard duty were
patched in to join in the razzing. They told Riedemann not to
worry, everyone on guard duty was watching and when the captain
brought me home they would let him know.

The next morning Riedemann reported to camp and found he had KP
duty. As he was peeling potatoes a 2nd lieutenant, who had also
heard the whole story, walked in and he too started razzing Riedemann. He told Riedemann that if he didn't quit trying to date the
captain's girl he would be peeling potatoes for the rest of the
war.

Riedemann laughed and said, "Well Lieutenant when my battery commander beats my time there isn't a thing I can do about it." Just
as he said that in walked the captain. Everyone started to laugh
and poor Riedemann was so embarrassed. He turned to the captain and
said, "Captain, wanna help me peel potatoes so I get out in time
for my date tonight?"

November 1943

Dear Mom and Dad,
I wish you could see me now, we've been transferred from the USO
club where we were to the most primitive camp you can imagine.
We're living in tarpaper barracks in the woods and have two coal
stoves for heat. I can't tell you the name of the town where we are
because we're now in the embarkation process.

Last Friday night before we left Sandston we gave a big Halloween party. There were about five times as many soldiers as we had
planned for; it was real experience to keep everything under control. I was in charge of entertainment and acted as Master of Cer-
emonies. I divided the crowd into four groups to compete against
each other in relay races.

First was a suitcase relay. There were four suitcases, each filled
with lingerie, nighties, housecoats, hair ornaments and anything
else collected from the girls. To begin I asked each group to send
up the man who knew the most about women; oh did they love that!
The teams came forward in a bunch but one GI on each team carried
their man on his shoulders. They were all shouting, "Here's our
boy."

I told them the girls had lost pieces of clothing and the MPs had
found them. Everything was now packed in these four suitcases. Then
I told the teams how the game would be played. I said, "You boys
have to put on whatever you find in your suitcase and race to the
finish line. The first team to have all its men at the finish line
wins."

It was a scream watching the fellows trying to figure out how to
get into women's lingerie and run a race. One 6'5" GI, who weighed
230 pounds, got a pair of panties from his suitcase. He could only
get them as far as his knees and had to race that way. Another got
my hair combs with the daisies and had to get them in his short,
GI hair before he could start running. One of the younger fellows

pulled a brassiere out of his suitcase and was really embarrassed because he didn't know how to get it hooked behind his back. The fellows in his group were screaming instructions and laughing 'til tears came.

The next game was jitterbug with GI Josephine. I made Josephine out of a mop that had a white string head. I braided the strings, tied red bows on the ends and made a girl's face out of crepe paper. It was pretty funny. This time I told the boys to pick out their very best jitterbug dancer and send him up. I said I had a pretty little girl from Charleston who had come to dance with them and with that I yelled, "Bring on GI Josephine." The fellows just howled when they saw that mop and watched the boys jitterbug with it. We had all sorts of silly stunts like that because the boys like to play silly games and laugh. It takes their minds off the war and makes them feel like kids again.

I wish I could've counted the number of boys who thanked us for the party. Said we couldn't know what it meant to them. If you could just meet some of the GIs who tell us how much they appreciate us being nice to them it would eat your heart out. One was a boy from Minnesota who had never been away from home; another boy's parents had died and he didn't have anyone left. I could go on and on. These boys are either preparing to ship out to the front or they are back on leave from the front. They're all scared. Some of the guys who've come back from the front tremble so much they can't hold a coffee cup. I'm so glad we can help them.

Eighteen months after this party took place LeOna was in Rome. The city had recently been liberated; thousands of Allied troops were there on leave. As LeOna walked down the Via Veneto, she heard someone call out to her. It was a young GI who said, "Hey you, aren't you the Red Cross girl who put on the party at Camp Patrick Henry before we shipped out?"

"Yes," she replied, "I am." The GI said, "Know how many guys from that outfit are left? Ten!"

There's a little white chapel in the woods that's always filled with service men. I've seen captains, majors and privates all kneeling together praying and taking Communion before they leave for the front. One captain held a picture of his wife and baby as

he prayed. Seeing that really makes you think.

Last night a gang of boys came in, really just young kids. They are shipping out today and were they scared. Many were thinking about whether this might be their last night in the United States because they were afraid they would be killed or captured. All they wanted to do was talk so I started chattering away about anything. I said they'd be fine and that we'd all meet in Cairo or someplace and have a party. I told them when we got back to the States I'd take them all fishing in Minnesota. The boys started to relax a little and next thing I knew they were planning the party in Cairo and the fishing trip in Minnesota.

Then I pulled out the songbooks and started singing, "There's a tavern in a town," and "Hail, Hail the gang's all here." We sang 'til everybody was laughing. I'm so happy to help in some small way. These boys can't fight if they are all mixed up and scared.

Big formations of bomber escorts just flew over so I suppose the boys are on their way. I pray they will be safe.

Above: recruitment posters circa 1942

December 1943

Dear Mom and Dad,
We've moved on from where we were last. Now we're on the Atlantic
seaboard making final preparations to leave. There's a pretty little chapel here with a beautiful pipe organ that has chimes. Every
evening they play hymns on the chimes, it's really beautiful. This
is a very solemn time for the boys, everyone prays a lot. I pray
too, mostly for them.

We had to ship our civilian clothes home today. From now on we're
only allowed to wear our uniforms. I sent almost everything to you
but I hid my darling cocktail skirt, silver lame blouse and black
patent leather heels with the ankle straps that I bought at Garfinkel's in Washington. I hid them in my bedroll because wherever in
the world I am on Christmas Eve I intend to wear that outfit.

This may be the last letter you get for a while.

LeOna Kriesel in uniform

MILITARY TRANSMISSION RECEIVED

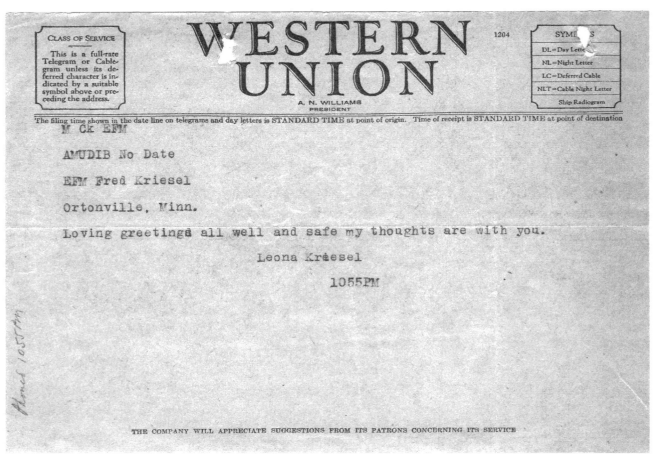

Loving greetings, all well and safe, my thoughts are with you.
LeOna

WESTERN UNION

A. N. WILLIAMS
PRESIDENT

1204

The filing time shown in the date line on telegrams and day letters is STANDARD TIME at point of origin. Time of receipt is STANDARD TIME at point of destination

10 SER

Washington D C 723PM Dec 1

Mr Frederick Kriesel

Ortonville, Minn.

Glad to announce safe arrival Leona Kriesel in north Africa

Ryan, Red Cross

747PM

North Africa
December 1, 1943

Mr. Frederick Kriesel,
Glad to announce safe arrival LeOna Kriesel in North Africa
Ryan, Red Cross

41

North Africa
December 1943

Dear Mom and Dad,
We're here, I can't believe I'm actually in a foreign country! I'm just thrilled. When the ship pulled into port I couldn't believe my eyes at what I was seeing. Arabs! Just like out of those pag-eants old Mrs. Duel used to put on when we were kids. They wore long, flowing robes and had turbans on their heads. Women had veils on their faces that reached all the way up to their eyeballs. They walked behind the men; lots of men were either leading or riding on camels. Oh what a sight it was!

Mrs. Duel's pageants were part of the annual Christmas celebration in Ortonville. The North African Arabs LeOna saw reminded her of the Three Wise Men.

As we pulled into port a military band welcomed us and Red Cross girls waited with donuts and coffee. I wish I could tell you exact-ly where in North Africa I am because you wouldn't believe it!"

In 1943, overseas travel was primarily the purview of privilege. Most people did not travel far from home; even fewer traveled to exotic lands with which they had no familial connection.

LeOna had grown up in southwestern Minnesota where most people were of Scandinavian or German descent. As she looked out at the North African Arabs she could hardly believe her eyes. It was so different from anything she had ever experienced.

In several letters she wrote about how dirty the Arabs were, how primitive their stores and transportation vehicles were. This was not meant to be pejorative. It was a fact of life in North Africa at the time. Money was scarce; the majority of Arabs lived in substandard conditions without the luxury of indoor plumbing.

On a picture in her scrapbook LeOna wrote, "Native quarters in Constantine, Algeria. Note lack of windows. Usually only light was through door. Sewage flowed along edge of walk, along building." She also noted, "Contrast Arab quarters with ultra modern apartments."

When we arrived we learned the army had been told to expect the soldiers but not the women. No one knew what to do with us. Finally it was decided we would be loaded up in army trucks and taken to the base until someone figured it out. Well, the trucks had small cabs in front where only two people could sit, the driver and an-other soldier. Everyone else had to ride in the open backs.

Native quarters in Constantine, Algeria —

Note lack of windows. Usually only light was through door.

Sewage flowed along edge of walk, along building.

Arab quarters, Constantine Algeria

(over)

Above:
Back of photo

Constantine
Algeria Arab Quarters

Constantine, Algeria

Driving through town I'd like to have twisted my neck off looking around. Everywhere I looked there were Arabs with camels and donkeys and women in long dresses with veils on their faces that went all the way up to their eyeballs. They carried big baskets full of stuff on their heads. There were Arabs driving horse-drawn vehicles we were told were taxis.

LeOna Kriesel with Arab man in Constantine, Algeria

None of us could believe what we were seeing. We all pointed at the Arabs and shouted to each other, "Look, Oh look at that!" I bet the Arabs thought we were quite a sight too. We were dressed in uniforms complete with steel helmets, haversacks and gas masks hanging from our pistol belts.

I can't tell you how beautiful it is here. Fences covered with purple flowers are everywhere; they look like what we have in the back yard. Looking out from the army camp reminds me of looking out across the lake at home so I don't feel very far away.

We're getting a big kick out of being at camp, eating out of mess kits and sleeping on the darndest beds you ever saw. The beds are actually little wooden frames with chicken wire stretched across the top. On top of the chicken wire are mattresses, really just sacks of awful-smelling straw. We each have four army blankets, no sheets or pillows. I'm using my field jacket as a pillow.

We expect to move on to Red Cross Headquarters soon and get our assignments. Everyone says we'll probably have to take a train to where we are going. From what I've heard about North African trains I think it would be more expedient to ride a camel.

NORTH AFRICA
AND THE
AMERICAN RED CROSS

Prior to the start of the war, northern Africa was dominated by imperialistic European powers. France controlled the western states of Morocco, Tunisia and Algeria plus most of the sub-Saharan area. Britain controlled Egypt, Sudan and Kenya. Italy held Libya and Ethiopia; all three controlled portions of Somalia.

In 1940, there were minor engagements in Ethiopia, Somalia and along the Mediterranean coast, but the real focus of the fighting was in Europe. However, after the failure of the German air war against Great Britain in late 1940, Hitler made plans to seize control of the Mediterranean and the Suez Canal, which would give the Axis powers (Germany, Italy and Japan) access to Middle Eastern oil.

From his base in Libya, Italian Marshall Rodolfo Graziani invaded Egypt and advanced about 50 miles into Egypt. British General Archibald Wavell counterattacked and drove the Italians nearly 400 miles back across Libya where he trapped and captured the majority of the Italian army near Benghazi in February 1941. Mussolini called for German help. In March 1941, the Luftwaffe began operations from Sicily, and General Irwin Rommel (known as the Desert Fox) and his German Afrika Corps arrived in Tripoli, Libya.

British forces were weakened because they had transferred several troops to defend Greece; Rommel moved rapidly to attack. By mid-April, Rommel had regained the Egyptian border and captured much of the British force. For the next 18 months, the opposing forces seesawed along the coastal road. First one would advance, then the other; the ability of each to advance was based largely upon the availability of reinforcements and supplies.

Finally in the summer of 1942, Marshall Rommel gathered sufficient forces to push 200 miles into Egypt, just 60 miles short of Alexandria. There the German/Italian offensive ground to a halt. Sensing the British strength was rapidly exceeding his, Rommel made a final assault on the British army, under the command of Lieutenant General Bernard Montgomery.

The assault failed. Reinforced now, and with air superiority, General Montgomery won the decisive battle of El Alamein, Egypt, in late October 1942. This began the long push that eventually drove Rommel out of Libya into Tunisia by February 1943.

While Rommel and Montgomery were fighting along the eastern coast, an allied invasion force under command of American General Dwight D. Eisenhower landed near Casablanca, Morocco. Smaller units landed in Algeria, at both Oran and Algiers. All three landings were resisted by Vichy French colonial troops but resistance ended quickly.

Combined American and British force in Algiers raced eastward to seize Tunis. Axis forces controlled the eastern half of Tunisia, Eisenhower's Allied forces held the western section; at the same time Montgomery's 8th Army moved in from Libya. By mid-May 1943 the remaining German and Italian units surrendered, thus ending an Axis presence in North Africa.

By December of 1943, when LeOna arrived, combat had moved in the direction of Tunis and Italy. Algeria was then a rear staging area, or logistical base, that supported the front. In this rear area, supplies were delivered and stockpiled, equipment fabricated and repaired, and arriving troops trained.

Soldiers from units that experienced heavy combat and loss at the front were sent to the rear area to rest and recuperate before they were sent into battle again. Red Cross clubs were located in the rear areas.

They were established throughout the world at the request of the United States government. At its peak, the Red Cross operated nearly 2,000 recreational service facilities abroad, staffed by 5,000 Red Cross workers and approximately 140,000 local volunteers.

It was a quasi-military organization in which overseas workers were given the honorary rank of officer to protect them in case of capture. The officer rank also allowed them to dine in the officer's clubs and enjoy rest and relaxation times in fancy hotels that offered rooms at substantially reduced rates to senior service personnel.

The American Red Cross was such an important organization that First Lady Eleanor Roosevelt and Senator Margaret Chase Smith championed their services. Red Cross recruiters sought out highly qualified young women, 27-years-old and older, who had college degrees and impeccable moral backgrounds. Once identified and recruited candidates were sent to Washington, D.C. for interviews.

Red Cross clubs offered a touch of home to lonely soldiers who often served many years overseas. Red Cross girls reminded them of mothers, sisters, wives and girlfriends left behind; they made the world a little smaller, a little safer. Many of the soldiers were just young boys drafted while still in high school. For most it was the first time they'd ever been away from home; now, all alone, they faced the most devastating combat in human history, World War II. They had seen buddies maimed, mutilated and killed. The possibility of the same happening to them was always on their minds. Fear was a constant companion.

Inside the Red Cross club there was life, happiness and fun. Soldiers danced, sang, laughed, had parties, celebrated holidays, played games, wrote letters, ate donuts and sandwiches, drank coffee by the gallons and talked. Often all they wanted was just to talk to an American girl; find out where she was from and if she knew anyone they knew. Red Cross girls felt that compassionate listening was their greatest gift.

English poet G.K. Chesterton wrote that men fight not because they hate what is in front of them but because they love what is behind them. Red Cross girls, American girls, reminded soldiers of what they were fighting for back home. It gave them the courage needed to keep fighting.

LeOna Kriesel with North African taxi

EXOTIC NORTH AFRICA

North Africa

Dearest Mom and Dad, Emmett and Babe:

We arrived yesterday after a very enjoyable t
They left us on the deck until we got in the harbo
and it certainly was a beautiful sight. I've never
been so thrilled in my life. We loaded in big open
trucks and were driven thru the city out to the cam
I'd like to have twisted my neck off looking at a
dirty Arab riding a little donkey on one side of the road,
a horse-drawn taxi on the other side, to Arabs with
camels behind us, women peeking thru veils on anoth
side. Guess you can just see all of us girls in our

The censors cut out the location

yelling "Look - oh look at this etc." The scenery was
fascinating. As yet I don't know how much of that I
can tell so will wait until we get more instruction
The flowers on the fences are beautiful. Some look like
that vine we have in the back yard with purple flowers
The view from our camp reminds me of home, lookin
across the lake so I don't feel very far away. I can
realize I'm in a foreign country.

If only you could realize how happy I am you
wouldn't worry. This is going to be one of the greatest
experiences in my life. The trip over on a transport
was so exciting. Now were getting a big kick out of
this camp, eating out of a mess kit, sleeping on the
darndest beds you ever saw. They have a little woode
framework with chicken wire for "springs." Our mattres
is a sack of straw and smells awful. We have fou
army blankets, no sheets or pillows. I use my field
jacket for a pillow.

The navy had a dance planned for us last
night. It was so cute the way the boys decorated
the hall with palm branches. They enclosed the
orchestra stand with palms and then hung palms
on the walls. It looked very pretty. They served
cheese and crackers. We
such a nice reception. It
dance they had ever had in this
hall so it was quite an occasion

Tuesday we get a pass to go to town. We are
hoping the boys we met on the boat will be
able to get out too because they plan to show
us around. There are six couples of us that had
such a wonderful time on the boat. My frien

Letter from North Africa:
note the censor cut out the location, Constantine

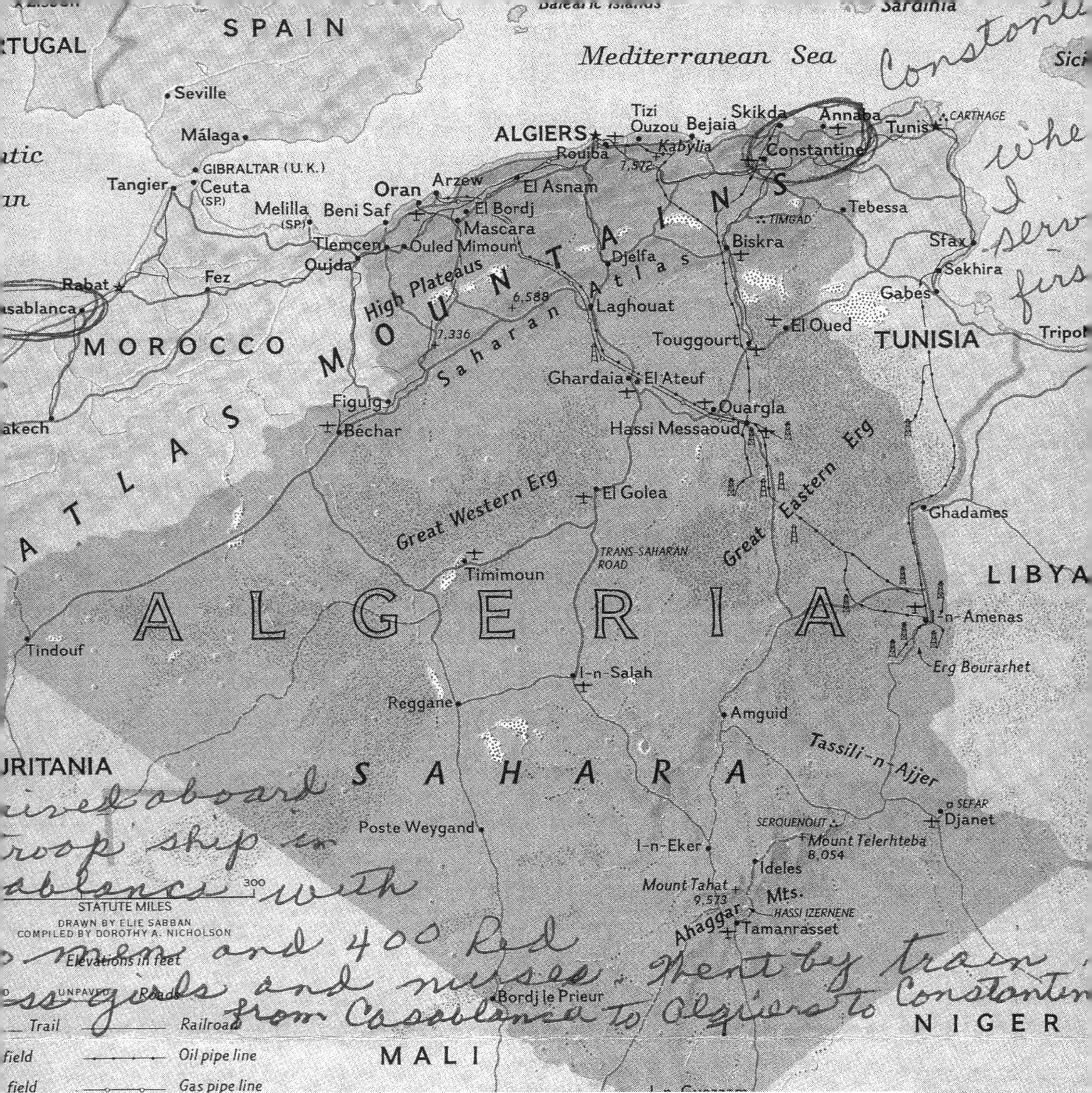

SPAIN

Mediterranean Sea

PORTUGAL

Seville

Málaga

Tangier
Ceuta (SP.)
GIBRALTAR (U.K.)
Melilla (SP.)

Rabat

Casablanca

Fez

MOROCCO

Tindouf

ALGIERS
Rouiba
Oran
Arzew
El Asnam
El Bordj
Mascara
Ouled Mimoun
Tlemcen
Oujda
Beni Saf

Tizi Ouzou
Bejaia
Kabylia
7,572

Skikda
Annaba
Constantine

Tunis
CARTHAGE

Tebessa
Sfax
Sekhira

Djelfa
Laghouat

Biskra
TIMGAD

Gabes

El Oued

TUNISIA

Tripoli

High Plateaus
6,588
7,336

ATLAS MOUNTAINS

Saharan Atlas

Touggourt

Figuig
Béchar

Ghardaia
El Ateuf

Ouargla

Hassi Messaoud

Great Eastern Erg

Ghadames

LIBYA

Great Western Erg

El Golea

TRANS-SAHARAN
ROAD

ALGERIA

I-n-Amenas

Erg Bourarhet

Timimoun

I-n-Salah

Reggane

Amguid

Tassili-n-Ajjer

MAURITANIA

SAHARA

Poste Weygand

I-n-Eker

Mount Tahat
9,573

SEROUENOUT
Mount Telerhteba
8,054
Ideles
Mts.
HASSI IZERNENE
Tamanrasset
Ahaggar

SEFAR
Djanet

STATUTE MILES
300
DRAWN BY ELIE SABBAN
COMPILED BY DOROTHY A. NICHOLSON
Elevations in feet

UNPAVED Road
Trail
Railroad
field Oil pipe line
field Gas pipe line

Bordj le Prieur

MALI

NIGER

Handwritten annotations:
Constantine
when I serv first
rived aboard troop ship in ablanca with men and 400 Red ...gials and nurses. Went by train from Casablanca to Algiers to Constantine
Rode n Casa onca to Algiers, left on Wed. & arrived

LeOna's own annotated map torn from the August 1973 National Geographic magazine that featured the area she served. Note the route she took between Casablanca and Constantine (both circled)

REVENUES from enormous Saharan petroleum fields fuel industrial expansion in Africa's second largest nation; after 1976 Algeria expects to be providing much of the natural gas consumed on the East Coast of the United States. Yet agriculture remains the major occupation, and 95 percent of the people crowd

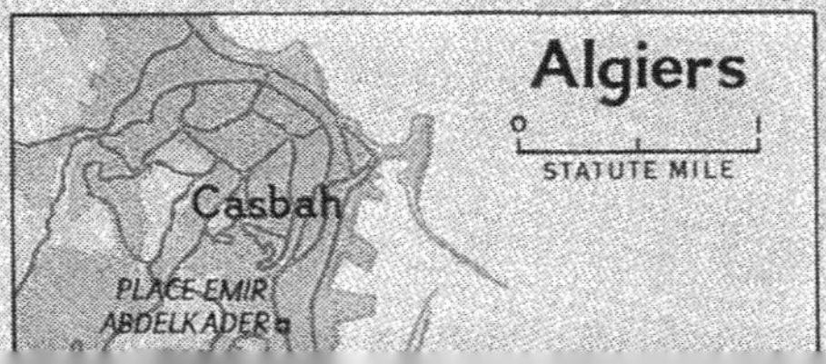

Algiers
Casbah
PLACE EMIR
ABDELKADER
STATUTE MILE

North Africa
December 1943

Dear Mom and Dad,
Some other Red Cross girls and I just completed a train trip across
North Africa. What an experience that was! We rode over 1,000 miles
to our first destination which took from Wednesday afternoon until Saturday night. Sunday, Irene Baumann and I changed to a faster
train and continued for another two days to our destination.

When we started we were seven girls plus luggage, in a compartment
about the size of an army blanket. After sitting up the first night
I suggested we make a "bed" by piling our bedrolls on the floor
between the two parallel benches. We drew straws to see who had to
sleep in the middle and guess who ended up with the short straw,
me! And here it had been my idea.

Four girls "slept" with their heads on one end; the other three
slept with their heads on the other end. That meant there were four
of us across with three pairs of feet between our heads. No one
could move unless someone said, "Shift." Then we all had to turn.
Oh Lordy, I thought I couldn't stand it from one night to the next
but after a couple nights you're so tired you can sleep any place.

The train stopped to pick up passengers at small villages along the
way. You can't believe what an assortment of people got on. Mostly
Arabs, each carried his belongings in a huge basket. When an Arab
woman with a live rooster on her shoulder got on we held the door
to our compartment shut so she couldn't come in and sit with us.
The woman was peeking over her veil looking into every compartment
for a place to sit. That rooster didn't even have a string on his
foot so she could hold onto him. We weren't taking any chances.

No one called out the stations when we stopped like they do in the
States, so every time one of us had to jump out and read the station sign to see where we were. The only thing we had to eat was
army "C" rations that were **always** meat and vegetable stew. Hot, the
stew was probably good but cold all I can say is that it was fill-

"C" rations were canned rations issued to the troops when fresh food, or packaged unprepared food, was not a practical option. There were only three main course meals offered as "C" rations, they included: meat and beans, meat and potato hash, or meat and vegetable stew. There was also a "C" ration for dessert. Official U.S. Library of Congress image.

ing. We also got three pieces of candy and what looked like three little dog biscuits. After eating the same thing three times a day for three days we were so sick of "C" rations we didn't know what to do.

I had been thinking about an idea and timing how long our stops were in each station. Each stop was between 30 and 45 minutes. I figured that was long enough for me to get out and find someone to trade their food for our "C" rations. I told the girls about my plan and asked who wanted to donate "C" rations. Well, everyone did.

The next time the train stopped off I went, my arms loaded with "C" rations. I had no idea where I was, somewhere in the Atlas Mountains. Not too far from the station I found a very primitive village, so primitive pigs were running around in the street! But there was a big hotel right in the middle of town and I figured that was a good place to start.

Luckily there was a French officer inside having lunch, he even spoke English. I told him about our predicament and asked if he would negotiate a trade, which he did. Speaking French to the Arabs and English to me the officer managed to trade our "C" rations for coffee, bread, cheese and sausages.

When I got back to the train there was still time for a little more bartering. I found the engineer and said if he'd give me some boiling engine water I'd give him a cup of coffee. He filled my helmet with hot water and I dumped in the Arab's ground coffee. I gave the engineer his share and took the rest back to the girls. When they smelled coffee and saw me with sausages, bread and cheese were they ever thrilled. Did we eat! Sandwiches and coffee never tasted so good. After that we traded at every stop. The Arabs took our "C" rations and we got their oranges.

Finally we arrived at the stop where five of the girls were getting off but Irene and I still had farther to go. The two of us changed trains and continued another two days. There was nothing on the train for us to eat and we were out of "C" rations and oranges. At the end of the first day we were starving. I said to Irene, "I have some candy bars in my suitcase and I saw where they put the baggage. I'm going to get out and run back to the baggage car and get those candy bars."

Irene cried, "Oh, you can't, what if the train starts going and I'm on here all alone?" I ignored her and jumped off the train. I raced to the baggage car and fortunately the door was open but it was pretty far up from the platform. I gave a real good jump and was halfway in the door, my legs and feet hanging out, as the train began to move. Just then someone stuck a gun in my face!

"Get that gun out of my face and pull me in," I shouted. "I'm an American Red Cross girl." The gun was in the hands of an English soldier guarding the luggage. He demanded to know what the heck I was doing. I told him Irene and I had been on a train for four days, had two more to go, and we were out of food. I said I had come to get candy bars out of my suitcase. Hearing this the soldier said we could have his biscuits and butter. He also said he'd help me get back to my cabin and see if he could find some more food.

When we finally arrived at our destination it was 10:00 p.m. and the station was closed. It was totally dark and no one was there to meet us. The English guard, who had now become our friend, said it was far too dangerous for us to be on the street alone after dark. He went to the engineer and told him to hold the train while he escorted us to the Red Cross club nearby.

When we got inside the club there was a beehive of activity. All Irene and I cared about was finding the bathroom. Someone directed us to the second floor and we headed straight up the stairs. A bunch of guys from the railway battalion heard us ask and knowing what was to come the whole group of them gathered at the bottom of the stairs to wait.

The bathroom was just one room with a hole in the floor. In front of the hole were two raised footprints; a long chain hung from the ceiling. Neither of us wanted to go back out in the dark hall so we took turns squatting over the hole. When we had both finished I pulled the chain and with that the entire floor flooded with water! Then it dawned on us what the footprints were for, had we stood on them our shoes wouldn't have gotten soaked.

Back down the stairs we came, shoes sloshing with water, to the absolute delight of the railway battalion boys. We learned it was a rite of passage and everyone loved watching "first-timers" as they came down the stairs with shoes full of water. A few months later those same railway battalion boys made Irene and me little ashtrays in the shape of the footprints. They said they wanted us to have a real souvenir!

North Africa
December 6, 1943

Dearest Mom and Dad:

I'm dashing this letter off very quickly as a Captain is making arrangements to get some letters off for us tonight that will reach you very quickly.

Please don't worry about me in the least. The army is taking such good care of us, we're becoming spoiled. They provide us with transportation all over. I've ridden in jeeps, weapon carriers, ambulances — everything but a horse drawn cart. The food is excellent. I'm eating like a little pig but we are always hungry in this climate.

The boys that we came with have shown us a wonderful time. They bought us a membership in the Automobile Club and we've been dancing every night. They have had three dances at their camp in the darlingest officers club. I'll describe it in a long letter I am typing. Ran into a gang of boys I knew on one of my Red Cross assignments in the States. They saw me right after they got in. You'd think we'd known each other all our lives, we were so tickled.

Look at the picture of the sign post in the October 30 Colliers. It amused me a lot to see it. Felt like home.

North Africa
December 1943

Dear Mom and Dad,
Irene and I are getting settled in our new home. We are sharing an apartment with two other Red Cross girls and it actually has hot water! This may sound funny to you but honest and truly it's such a luxury for us we're just thrilled.

Today we took a tour of the town and even got inside a mosque. In the Arab quarters we saw men with their harem of Muslim women. I'll write all about that in my next letter, must go to bed now so I can get up early to-morrow and shop for Christmas. This place is so interesting I don't want to miss a thing. I'm gaining weight because the army feeds us really well. In fact, I have nothing but the highest praise for the way they're taking care of us.

apt. where I lived a few months

Constantine, Algeria

Merry Christmas! I'll be thinking about you a lot!

December 1943

Dear Mom and Dad,
I like my job very, very much. Guess I'm about one of the happiest girls you could find. The boys have nicknamed me "laughing girl." I'm having so much fun I can't help but laugh all the time.

We've had the GIs making Christmas decorations out of absolutely nothing. Wish you could see them making chains out of brightly colored construction paper; they're just like little kids. We painted old ping-pong balls and hung them on the tree for ornaments and

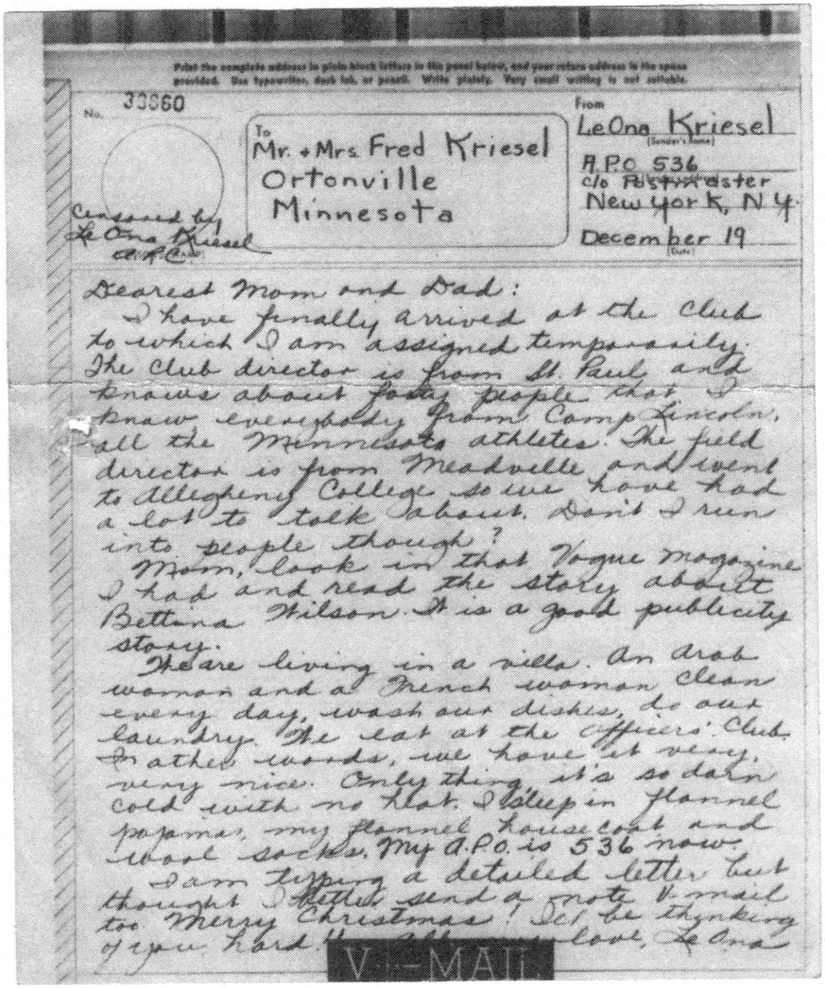
No. 33060

To
Mr. + Mrs. Fred Kriesel
Ortonville
Minnesota

From
LeOna Kriesel
A.P.O. 536
c/o Postmaster
New York, N.Y.
December 19

Censored by
LeOna Kriesel
A.R.C.

Dearest Mom and Dad:
I have finally arrived at the Club to which I am assigned temporarily. The Club director is from St. Paul and knows about forty people that I know everybody from Camp Lincoln, all the Minnesota athletes. The field director is from Meadville and went to Allegheny College so we have had a lot to talk about. Don't I run into people though?
Mom, look in that Vogue magazine I had and read the story about Bettina Wilson. It is a good publicity story.
We are living in a villa. An Arab woman and a French woman clean every day, wash our dishes, do our laundry. We eat at the Officers' Club. In other words, we have it very, very nice. Only thing, it's so darn cold with no heat. I sleep in flannel pajamas, my flannel housecoat and wool socks. My A.P.O. is 536 now.
I am typing a detailed letter but thought I better send a note V-mail too. Merry Christmas! I'll be thinking of you. hard ... love, LeOna

V-MAIL

V-mail: shown actual size

we've made stars out of tin can tops. The boys used the cellophane from cigarette boxes to make little stockings and we filled them with candy.

Everything looks really cute but you should see our tree. It's a scroungy little North African pine tree that some nice person cut down and dragged to the club for us. The tree even has lights, thanks to the boys from the signal corps.

Tonight we had a Christmas pageant here at the club. It's so cold I could see my breath but it's Christmas Eve and I'm wearing that outfit from Garfinkel's. When the other Red Cross girl came into the club, dressed in her uniform, overcoat and snow boots, she saw me all dolled up and whined, "You're not allowed to be out of uniform."

I don't care; the boys just love seeing an American girl dressed up like an American girl. I played the piano and we all sang Christmas carols. Tomorrow we're having a dance at the club in the afternoon and in the evening we're having the wounded soldiers up to our villa for dinner.

Guess what, I got a Christmas present! Yesterday the boys must have heard me say I wouldn't have any presents this year and today I found a little package on my desk. It was all wrapped up and the card read, "Merry Christmas to LeOna, from the MPs." Inside was a chicken sandwich. One of the boys had saved his chicken from dinner and made me that sandwich as a present. Gosh, you just can't imagine how nice these boys are to us. One who works in the railway shop is from Texas. He made me a coffee pot, frying pan and kettle. I said something about cooking everything in a canteen cup and he went right back to the shop and made me cooking utensils.

January 1943

Dear Mom and Dad,
Did you have a good Christmas? I had a swell time. I went to the captain's house for a party on Christmas Eve. He made eggnogs out of canned milk, which were quite good. Under the tree he had home-made cookies, fudge and dates. Seemed almost like Christmas Eve at home.

At midnight we went to mass at a big Catholic church. It was beautiful. As we drove the jeep to church we could hear the bells ringing; they sounded so beautiful coming through the mountains I got a tingly feeling. Inside the church a wonderful choir of Welsh soldiers sang Christmas carols. It was all like something out of a movie.

Christmas day the director of our club, Ben, took another girl and me to dinner at the French home of someone he knows. Don't think I'll ever go to another French dinner. They drink wine like water and think everyone else should too. The host and four of the guests could "no comprendre" English and of course Ben, the other girl and I could "no comprendre" French.

The evening began with much handshaking and a glass of white wine, followed by a glass of red wine. The first course consisted of two huge pieces of salmon loaf, served with more white wine. The second course consisted of hard-boiled eggs that were served with muscatel. Third was creamed celery, served with claret. Kriesel learns the word "non" and screams it as the host said, "Encore," and poured more wine.

Fourth course was a green salad with ripe olives; I'm afraid I insulted our host when I flatly refused another glass of wine. Ben apologized and tried to make amends speaking his broken French with a touch of English. He said, "Mademoiselle LeOna uh-uh sell-ee-brate—comprendre? Jolly Noel Eve. Ah wee, wine, whiskey, comprendre? Mademoiselle sig sag. Non can drink more." I couldn't believe Ben was telling our host I had gotten drunk the night before! I said, "Ben Stoddard, that's an awful thing to say! You know very well I went to church Christmas Eve." He replied, "Shut up, shut up, everything's okay. Hadda tell him something."

So the last course came and it was a beautiful French pastry in the shape of a Yule log. Right behind it comes the maid, Suzanne, with two bottles of champagne! At that point poor Kriesel was drunk and wondered if the table would stand still long enough to get hold of the pastry.

After two glasses of bubbling champagne were served we had oranges, tangerines and fresh dates. I thought that was "finis," but no! Our host brought out lovely little silver glasses and poured a shot of something that tasted like cocoa. At that point I decided one or two more wouldn't make any difference so I let 'er go down the hatch.

After some more hand-shaking and "Merci Beaucoup" we got our coats on but weren't allowed to leave until we had a small glass of whiskey. Oh mother, mother, 'twas a great Christmas.

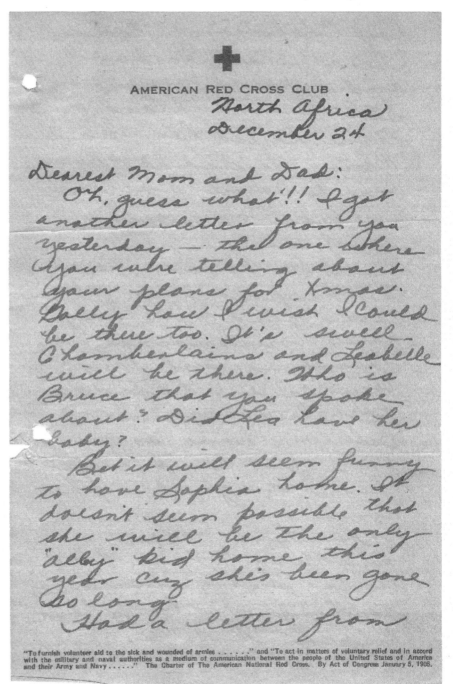

AMERICAN RED CROSS CLUB

North Africa
December 24

Dearest Mom and Dad:
Oh, guess what!! I got another letter from you yesterday — the one where you were telling about your plans for Xmas. Golly how I wish I could be there too. It's swell Chamberlains and Isabelle will be there. Who is Bruce that you spoke about? Did Lea have her baby?

Bet it will seem funny to have Sophia home. It doesn't seem possible that she will be the only "alby" kid home this year cuz she's been gone so long.

Had a letter from

January 1944

Dear Mom and Dad,
It's very, very cold here, nothing like I imagined Africa
to be. It's raw, damp and penetrating. When we get home
at night we shiver just trying to get undressed. I wear
long underwear, flannel pajamas and wool socks to bed. We
fill our canteens with boiling water and take them to bed;
there aren't any sheets so we sleep between army blankets.
We don't have pillows either. Can't you just see me trying
to get out of bed in the morning? Egad it's torture. These
houses have tile floors without any rugs. If you can imagine anything colder on your feet in an unheated house than
tile I'd like to know what it is.

Every morning we take a sponge bath in lukewarm water. You
can see your breath in the bathroom. I shake so much my
fillings are about to fall out!

You must wonder what we do about meals. We pay $10 ev-
ery two weeks for food and club privileges at a big hotel
that's been turned into an officer's mess. We have fairly
good food there and I'm getting fat. But we never have
coffee, fresh milk, eggs, fresh vegetables or butter. We
have grape jelly and peanut butter and lots of noodles and

macaroni. I can't get away from macaroni even in Africa. God bless it.

We have "C" rations a lot, mostly the same vegetable and meat stew we had on the train. We have Spam about 40 different ways and we have lots of pudding, dates and tangerines for dessert. Once in a while we're really lucky and have roast beef from the States.

Our social life is limited mostly to the club. We work from 9:30 a.m. - 12:00 p.m. Take an hour for lunch and then we're back at work from 1:00 - 6:00. Another hour for dinner and back again at 7:00 p.m. until 9:00 p.m. I have Thursday and Friday mornings off. We have dances at the club every Monday, Wednesday and Friday nights and boy, do we get a workout. All the boys want to dance with an American girl.

On Sunday we have church at 11:00, a matinee and bingo at 6:00. At 7:00 we have a musical program with some sort of community sing-a-long. Saturday nights we put on a stage show that's like a quiz program. It's GIs versus the WACs. Every Thursday night there's an officer's dance at the hotel.

Page spread image: Spam slices

LeOna with Fred Corcoran,
Jack Sharkey and
Lefty" Gomez

Next page:
USO party invitation

Constantine, Algeria

January 1944

Dear Mom and Dad,
We've had some celebrities here. Had my picture taken with Jack
Sharkey, the boxer, Lefty Gomez, the baseball pitcher, and Fred
Corcoran, the golfer. They were touring army camps when I met them.
We had dinner together and afterwards I went to a dance at the officer's club with Sharkey (the boxer) and a lieutenant. Dancing
with Jack Sharkey was an experience. If anyone bumped into him he
didn't move an inch. It was like dancing with a big tank but he was
very light on his feet.

Jack Sharkey, a bantering, cocksure boxer captured the world heavyweight championship in an unlikely victory over Max Schmeling in 1932.

Sharkey boxed professionally for 13-years during the Golden Age of Boxing. His year-long reign as heavyweight champion was the climax of an outstanding career.

Vernon Lewis "Lefty" Gomez, was one of the great pitchers of his day. He played for the New York Yankees from 1930 – 1942 and was named All Star in 1933, 1934, 1935, 1936, 1937, 1938 and 1939.

In 1936, Fred Corcoran, was the business manager for Sam Snead, one of the world's foremost golfers for most of four decades. During his career Corcoran had been an American sports promoter, agent, administrator and amateur golfer. He also served as tournament manager for the Professional Golf Association Tours.

I took the 3 special guests USO Party *to the Officers' Club to a dance.*
Special Guests:
Fred Corcoran, golfer
(3rd from left)
Le Cox (5th from left)
Jack Sharkey, boxer
(6th from left)
"Lefty Gomez", baseball
1/10/1944 (8th from left)

Thursday I'm going for a drive with another officer. We're going to a historical place with old Roman ruins including a Roman amphitheater and Roman roads. I'm excited to go. He's getting a picnic packed up at the hotel so we can really make a day of it.

The British officers have invited me to a party they're giving this week but I'm not going. Their dances are dull.

February 1944

Dear Mom and Dad,
Guess what! This morning I had a hot bath in a tub. Oh it was wonderful. I splashed around for half an hour, soaped up twice and then just soaked some more. Honestly, I feel like a new person. Funny what a luxury a bath is when you don't get one very often. One night last week we had butter at dinner. That was such a treat I ate big pieces of it on my potatoes. I know this sounds silly but that tub bath with hot water and the butter are perhaps the two most exciting things that have happened to me.

In this letter I thought I'd give you a sample of "My Day" with apologies to Eleanor Roosevelt.

Eleanor Roosevelt's "My Day" was a syndicated newspaper column published from 1935 to 1962.

8:00 a.m: Got up, took a sponge bath and got dressed

9:30: Arrived at the club. Had coffee and donuts with the MPs

10:00 - 12:00: Straightened up the game room, put out newspapers dated November 15, that had just arrived; answered the phone and gave callers the names of shows we'll be having here at the club. Made a sign for Sunday night's community sing; had a conference with a colonel who had the waist and hip measurements of some French lady. Told him what sizes to order in panties, bras, girdle, slip, dress and hose. Boy was he embarrassed!

Then four boys wanted to sniff my neck because they're lonesome for the smell of an American girl wearing good perfume. Took a transient officer back to a dressing room behind the stage where he could wash and shave. Checked out some library books. Took a telephone message for Private Hoffman, from an English captain who said, "Will you please have him give me a tinkle at 18:00 when he arrives?" Laughed for ten minutes at that message.

12:00: I climbed into a Red Cross car and went to the hotel for lunch. Twenty Arab shoeshine boys surrounded me saying, "Shine, Mees-American? Polish? What's cookin' Mees?" I shook the kids loose by promising the dirtiest one in the lot he can give me a shine after lunch.

Car wouldn't start, gave it a shove down the hill; barely missed two Frenchmen who were wearing horn-rimmed glasses, navy berets, golf knickers and plaid socks. These Frenchmen always walk in the street and never look where they're going.

Ate lunch consisting of Spam fried in egg batter, potatoes, creamed carrots, bread with grape jelly, water and half a peach floating around in lots of juice.

1:00 - 6:00: Back to club. Got shoes shined. Looked at picture of soldier's baby son. Sewed on a button. Played piano for two hours. Helped with inventory. Soldier brought in a new puppy for me to name; he seems to find a new puppy every day and brings it in for me to name. This one we named Pug Nose, Puggy for short. Took about 14 telephone calls from soldiers who just wanted to visit.

Dilbert, who is quite obese and a romanticist, told me I have beautiful eyes. Phillip wonders how I comb my hair in an up-sweep. "Curly" Holmes tells me how much the boys appreciate the fact I always look well groomed. So it goes, one compliment after another from boys that are just plain homesick for American girls.

One boy (a Section Eight) shows me plans for a house he's designing for his mother. It's modeled after the Queen Mary, complete with decks, and portholes for windows.

Someone read me a murder story he's writing and asked me to suggest a title. Hoffman brought 15 eggs that were packed in a tin can filled with straw. Len came back with my uniform he had dry cleaned in airplane fuel. Clarence brought me a bottle of Canadian ale he appropriated from the British. MP shows me the souvenirs he bought for his sister; helped him wrap the packages.

Section Eight is a designation given to soldiers evaluated as mentally unfit for combat.

6:00 - 7:30: For exercise I walked to the hotel for dinner. Ate dinner and returned to club for dance.

9:00: All pooped out, time to go home. MPs gave me a ride so the Arabs wouldn't get me. That's all for now.

FALLING IN LOVE
HE SAYS WE'LL MARRY

Lieutenant John J. Cox

March 1944

Dear Mom and Dad,
I'm dating a very nice boy. He's a first lieutenant from Boston.
At Syracuse University he was a fraternity brother of Dr. Talley,
president of Allegheny College where I taught. He was also a very
good friend of Bud Wilkinson, the University of Minnesota football
coach who was at Camp Lincoln when I was. Bud was coaching at Syracuse and that's where he and Johnny became friends. Johnny is an
Irish boy and full of fun.

This is the first mention of "Johnny." LeOna dropped a bombshell when she hinted at a serious relationship. Johnny was Italian on his mother's side, and half English and half Irish on his father's. Plus he was Catholic. The staunchly Methodist Nettie Jones Kriesel, of Welsh descent, did not view any of this news kindly.

Bud Wilkinson helped lead the Minnesota Golden Gophers to three consecutive National Championship titles from 1934 – 1936. He later became head coach for the University of Oklahoma Sooners and coached them to a 47 game winning streak from 1953 – 1957, an NCAA Division 1 record that still stands today.

LeOna and Wilkinson worked together at Camp Lincoln in Lake Hubert, Minnesota. Bud Wilkinson was a coach of the University of Minnesota football team at the time and brought the entire team with him to Lake Hubert. LeOna loved to tell how hard Bud made them work; her favorite recollection was of Bud making the team use their shoulders to push an old Ford through the sand.

She also loved her story about the time she and Bud dyed a bunch of sheep green. Whatever for will always remain a mystery.

It was a coincidence that Bud was the assistant football coach at Syracuse University where Johnny (John) Cox was a baseball player and captain of the boxing team.

He's one of the most popular officers here. Everybody likes him;
he's always laughing and full of fun. He has such nice manners I'm
proud to be with him. His mother sent him a newspaper clipping that
was in the Boston paper. I'm sending the picture to you in this
letter so you can see what he's like. I've got a hunch you'll be
seeing lots of him someday so I hope you like his looks.

Yesterday I went out to a railway battalion camp to get my teeth
checked. The dentist's office was in a tent with a wooden framework
for a door. The sloping part of the tent roof was cut away to allow
light to enter; a little iron chair sat in the doorway facing the
light. It was sort of cloudy when I first got there so we had to

"Johnny"

wait until the sun came out before the dentist could do his examination.

The railway battalion boys had made the dental equipment in their shop. It was so funny; the chair was nothing more than a steel stool with a pipe on it. At one end of the pipe was a headrest. They built a steel framework around the chair to hold the drill apparatus; there was a little arm with a little tray on it for the tools. A second arm held a coffee can to spit in.

LeOna quickly changes the subject. She probably knew this news of Johnny wasn't going down well.

The dentist found a cavity but the sun had moved behind the clouds. We had to wait until it came out again before he could fix it. When the sun finally came out the dentist said, "Turn on the power sergeant." The sergeant started pedaling a bicycle like mad and the drill went to beat the dickens.

When he finished the dentist started teasing me, said it was good to work on a mouth with lipstick again. He told me I was the first girl patient he'd had since he came into the army. A bunch of soldiers were in the back of the tent waiting for their shots, they just howled when they heard that!

Don't worry about me having to put up with anything. I'm having the time of my life and living very comfortably. Course after next week I don't know where I'll be because Irene and I might be transferred; so far it's swell.

April 1944

Dear Mom and Dad,
Haven't heard anything from you in a long time; hope I get a letter soon. Yesterday Johnny and I went to the Mediterranean, it was a swell trip.

The Arab villages we drove through were quite interesting, you can't imagine what they look like. The "downtown" section is usually about two blocks long. The buildings are constructed of something that looks like concrete painted white or cream. Instead of having separate stores, as we have, one building runs for about a block. Store fronts consist of two wooden or steel doors that slide up like garage doors. Counters start about five feet in from the door and run all the way through the store. There aren't any windows so the only light is what comes in through the doors making it very dark. There are oranges, tangerines, dates and vegetables piled every which way; it all looks dark and clammy.

Several grand hotels and resorts functioned as officer rest camps during World War II. Red Cross girls were also permitted to stay in these hotels and resorts. This was the 1940's; propriety was expected and respected.

Usually there's a roof held up with posts running the entire length of the building that makes kind of a front porch. Arabs, both men and women, squat under this roof all day long. I saw several Arab women with ragged, black cloaks draped around them and veils on their faces. They carry babies on their backs which really tickled me. You should see those kids hang on, even little bitty ones know enough to hang on for all they're worth. The kid puts his feet around the mother's waist and hangs on to her elbows, she locks her hands behind the baby's fanny. We saw lots women squatting in front of the stores with babies on their backs.

The men look like something from one of Mrs. Duel's pageants. They wear "white" turbans and yards and yards of material draped around their bodies in a cape effect. This material can be anything: white, hand-woven wool or striped mattress covers the Arabs get from American soldiers. Sometimes they wear capes made of burlap and sometimes their capes are made from a dirty orange material that looks like burlap. Usually they are barefoot, if not they wear homemade sandals. They almost always carry a crooked cane. Bunches of them squat in the dirt for hours; oh yes, I almost forgot, most of the women wear big, heavy silver bracelets with bells around their ankles. Those bracelets certainly produce a colorful effect, especially since the women are usually barefoot.

The Mediterranean is a beautiful sight. We drove along a road built on top of a retaining wall right next to the water. The ocean was terribly rough that day; as we drove along a breaker came in so fast it washed right over the car. That's when we turned around and started back. There were big, beautiful villas high up on the rocky cliffs overlooking the sea. It all seemed like something out of a dream.

Last night and this morning we had a typical Minnesota snowfall, something NOT typical in North Africa. One lady said it has been twelve years since they've had anything like this. Oh how I loved it! Put on my wool slacks and snow boots this morning and went hiking. Had a snowball fight with some Arab kids who couldn't figure out what it was all about. Oh how they'd laugh. When I got to the hotel the officers all ganged up on me, throwing snowballs and pushing me into the snow. This afternoon the sun came out and the snow is nearly gone. I'm so disappointed because Johnny promised to go hiking in the snow with me tonight.

Our club closed yesterday and we can't move into our new one yet so I have a little free time. I could go on indefinitely but I'll save some for next time.

Please write soon. No mail for two weeks from you.

April 1944

Dear Mom and Dad,
Johnny had his picture taken and gave me one to send you. Hope you like it! These photographers aren't like the ones at home. They snapped it while Johnny was talking to me. He said, "Your folks will think I haven't any teeth but assure them I have."

He's asked me to marry him as soon as we get back to the States and I've accepted.

The Kriesels had not acknowledged the previous letter from their daughter telling about "Johnny." Now she went one step farther and told them he had proposed. They were not happy about the news, and despite LeOna's pleading they never relented. She did everything she could to assure her parents this wasn't just a wartime romance. The Kriesels weren't budging. The Coxes, on the other hand, and their friends the Goodwins, were thrilled.

Johnny says I'm everything he ever wanted in a girl and the funny part of it is, that's exactly the way I feel about him. He said he'd be proud to take me to his home and I'd be just as proud to introduce him to you. He has a wonderful personality. He's very kind, a perfect gentleman, well educated and likes the same things I do: Sports, good music and good plays. He's very cultured.

He's begun saving $125 a month so when we get married I can have a really nice home. He's already saved around $3,000. I've decided not to waste my money on junky old souvenirs here and will send home as much money as I can, please save it for me. I'll want to buy nice silver and those Spode dishes because Johnny says we'll never waste money renting a house. His father told him he'd help him build a home whenever he got married. His family has a two-family home in Haverhill, Massachusetts and another home at the beach in New Hampshire.

We want to get married as soon as we get back home. However if the war lasts too long, we'll be married over here. I'd prefer to be married when you could be there but if this lasts too long I hope you'll forgive us. I know you'll both love Johnny as much as I do. He's really tops. He's in personnel so he has a swell position as far as the war is concerned. His papers are in now for the captaincy. That'll probably take a little time yet.

The Red Cross man is here talking about our new club. He said Irene and I will take full charge of it. We're thrilled because we don't want to leave here. We know everyone and it feels like home. We eat with the officers and have such a good time with them. They treat us like sisters. Irene and I will now be the only two American girls in town.

Please write, I haven't heard from you for going on three weeks.

April 1944

Dear Mom and Dad,
So toast and powder blue are this year's spring colors back in the States? Over here it'll be quite different. For the North African Easter parade mattress covers and tablecloths will be in vogue. Wooden clogs with straps across the insteps are also popular. Easter bonnets made of colorful, frayed rags draped in a turban effect will be in evidence on Rue Caraman (our 5th Avenue). I haven't decided what I'll wear yet.

Irene and I have been so busy today. I bought $9 worth of flowers so now we have flowers all over the club. Wish you could see the beautiful lilies we have here. The boys seem so pleased with the flowers, they've commented about them all day. We're going to color eggs in a few minutes. Tomorrow I'm going to try to borrow the little organ from the chaplain and play it here in the afternoon. We thought it'd be nice to have some organ music for Easter.

I had a very nice 28th birthday. The sergeants at the hotel where we eat baked me the biggest, three-layered chocolate cake I've ever seen. Johnny arranged with my landlady to have a little surprise party after the club closed. A gang of MPs and some other boys chipped in and gave me a beautiful ring. It has a purple stone that's set in sterling silver. They were so cute about it and said, "Now you're engaged to the gang of us. Don't be stepping out on us."

Last night I was fixing Easter baskets with colored eggs and a gang of boys helped. This morning I found a yellow egg in one basket with the following words written on it, "I'm LeOna, a good egg." That tickled me so much. By noon all of the eggs had disappeared from the baskets. I saw one boy sticking an egg into his pocket, he said, "Gee, Easter eggs. Just like back home."

Hot mineral water pool

The swimming pool opened and it's the most beautiful sight I've ever seen. Steep, rocky cliffs surround the pool; waterfalls come down the cliffs and right into the pool. The water is a beautiful blue because it comes from hot mineral springs. The pool is enormous, I was swimming last week and it was wonderful. Once a week it gets cleaned. Americans and British get to swim the first three days after cleaning, then the French have it the next four days.

There's a beach club, actually a stucco building, where wine and light refreshments are sold. We hope to have an orchestra out there soon.

Above and Left:
Constantine, Algeria swimming pool

AS TIME GOES BY

May 1944

Dear Mom and Dad,
I had to move again as my landlady's husband came home and brought
his sister. I'm in the same beautiful apartment building, just next
door to where I had been living. Three soldiers carried all my stuff
into the apartment. Johnny came over after work and unpacked, he
even hung up my clothes. Sometimes I feel like a regular ornament.
Honestly, I don't even put on my own overshoes. Somebody always does
that for us.

My apartment is actually just one room but it's quite large and
lovely. There are mosaic tiles on the floor, big French doors that
open out onto a curved balcony and French windows that open up just
like the French doors. I have a double bed with two mattresses and
nice white sheets. There's a glass-top desk, three chairs, a night
table and a big wardrobe with three doors. I get hot water (well
supposedly it's hot, we'd call it tepid) on Saturday and Sunday.

I'm living with a French lady and her two daughters. The daughters
are both schoolteachers. Every morning the lady brings me a little
pot of Arabic coffee with toast made out of black bread or sometimes French pastries instead of toast. She brings everything on a
big copper tray and says, "Bon Jour Mademoiselle, café?" Of course
I can't drink that Arabic coffee so I drive myself crazy trying to
think of a way to get rid of it but make it look as though I consumed the whole pot. This morning I tip toed into the bathroom and
poured it down the sink when she left to open the front door.

Oh Dad, I've meant to tell you about the Arab funerals; they are
so funny you'll get a kick out of hearing about them. One Arab
walks ahead of the procession with a board hanging around his neck,
there's some Arabic writing on the board. He's followed by four of
the dirtiest, most ragged pallbearers you could imagine. They are
usually dressed in gunnysack cloaks that have pointed hoods. Everyone's clothes are so ragged that even the patches are patched. They
all walk barefoot and their feet look like leather.

The corpse, covered with brightly colored silk, lies on a wooden
frame suspended on two wooden poles. The four pallbearers rest the

poles on their shoulders. Following along behind the corpse are from ten to thirty Arabs, all walking. Women, who are also walking, bring up the rear. The women wail whether or not they even knew the dead person. I hear that if you're rich you can hire lots of women to wail.

If it's a baby that died they carry the baby on a pillow. There seems to be a funeral of one kind or another every day at 1:30 p.m.

The worst I saw was a woman's funeral. Her body was covered with the silk cloth but her arms had been pulled out from under the cloth and folded on her chest. If you can believe it her fingernails were painted purple!

Constantine, Algeria 1944

The funerals sort of gagged me at first but now I'm getting used to them.

Well, I've got to get ready for dinner so 'bye' for now. Am anxious to hear what you think of Johnny when you get the picture. He sent a picture of me home to Boston today.

LeOna on hunting trip with Johnny
and the Catholic priest

May 1944

Dear Mom & Dad,

We're very busy getting a new club fixed up. That's why I haven't written as often this past week. Just finished scrubbing all the chairs and tables. Painted furniture yesterday and went so fast I almost felt an urge to paint a basement. Ha ha! Will try to take some pictures of our new club and send to you.

We're having the best time. Our latest acquisition is a German command car that we'll use to haul supplies. The car doesn't have a top and it's the craziest looking thing. When we take the car out, Gordon (a fellow who works in the club) and Irene sit in the front seat; I ride on a box in the back just in front of the spare tire. We sit so high we can look out all over the city. Needless to say, we attract a lot of attention!

Yesterday as we climbed in the car a little French kid, about 8-years-old, looked at us all wide-eyed, his mouth open, and said, "GERMANS?" "Ja," I said! Boy did he run for home. Bet he had a wild tale to tell his parents.

When we cruise up to the hotel for meals in our command car the officers get the biggest kick out of it. A major is going to take our picture so maybe I can send you one. The other day I had several errands to do so I took one of the cars from our Red Cross fleet. It's an old Studebaker someone got out of a salvage dump. Wherever I went people pointed at me and laughed. I thought they got a kick out of the car but it was me they were laughing at. Over here women don't drive cars and I guess they thought I looked queer.

I'm anxious to hear what you think of Johnny. Did you get the pictures yet? He's taking me to the jeweler this afternoon to get my finger measured. He's written his brother to pick out a diamond and is giving it to me as a belated birthday gift. I know you'll like him very, very much. He's really a gentleman.

May 1944

Dear Mom and Dad,
Have to tell you about another funeral I saw just the other day.
This one was real ritzy. It started off with about 150 little girls
dressed in navy blue uniforms. Mourners carried a big piece of
black cloth with gold fringe around the edges. Behind the mourners
there was a big, open carriage with nobody in it. Behind that was
another big carriage, this one had the inside covered with white
silk and silver fringe. The horses wore white blankets with silver
tassels on all four corners.

However it was the carriage driver who stole the show. He sat up
high all decked out in a dirty black uniform decorated with silver braids. He had tall boots on his feet and a big black hat with
white plumes on his head. Honestly, he looked like Napoleon.

Next came all the French women from town. Two other groups of
mourners followed them and carried big black cloths with gold
fringe. After that came about 20 little choirboys dressed in bright
red cloaks with white lace sleeves. The boys were chanting; they
were followed by three priests all decked out in colorful lace
dresses and little black hats with red pom-poms. The priest in
the middle carried a big stick with a Crucifix on it. Behind the
priests was yet another carriage, this one filled with flowers. All
the people in town followed the final carriage so it was quite a
display. The fanciest funeral I've seen!

May 1944

Dear Mom & Dad,

I'm sending you some pictures Johnny and I took when we were out hunting. That Arab kid in the picture was running around the fields so we had him pose with us. Look carefully at his shoes; they're pieces of leather tied onto his feet with twine. This kid is quite well dressed. Notice the crooked cane he has on his arm.

Last Friday, on my day off, Johnny and I took a trip to the Mediterranean. He brought breakfast from the hotel to my house. He's so good to me he spoils me. It was a swell trip. The mountains are all in bloom; almond trees are covered with pink blossoms and the grass is very green. There are daisies, hyacinths, jonquils, violets and something lavender that look like crocus. It looked so much like southern Minnesota in the spring that I got a little homesick.

LeOna with Arab boy

Did you get my letters telling about Johnny? You never mention anything about him. Johnny is everything I ever wanted in a man and you know I'm doggone particular! He is so thoughtful and kind.

There may be a possibility that Johnny will be sent back to the States in a few months because he's been over here so long. If that happens he plans to go home and see his parents and then he wants to come see you. I'll come home as soon as my time here is up and then we can be married in the States.

May 1944

Dear Mom and Dad,
I was interested to read about the war in the newspapers from
the States. I don't know anything about the South Pacific but
it certainly sounds encouraging, don't you think? From all in-
dications it would seem we're tearing along in Italy just like
the Morrison boys' basketball team.

We're having so many soldiers in our club everyday I'm pooped
out by the time 9:00 p.m. arrives. Last night a group of British soldiers put on a variety show that was really good. They
decked themselves out in cowboy costumes, strummed guitars and
sang American cowboy songs with their English accents. Think
that tickled us more than anything.

Did I tell you the GIs have mascots? One is a little boy from
Quebec whose father smuggled him here on a Canadian troop ship.
When the father moved out for combat he couldn't take the little boy along so the railway battalion boys adopted him. He's
about ten years old and as cute as can be. He is very well man-
nered and speaks English fluently.

The boys dress him like a little GI, they had uniforms cut down
to fit him. He even has leggings and a garrison cap. He comes
into town on a pass just like the soldiers, pulls KP duty and
gets his shots with the GIs. He really knows army discipline
and executes as snappy a salute as any soldier. It's so cute to
see how the GIs baby him. They fuss over him and take such good
care of him; he's always scrubbed and his clothes are always
clean and pressed.

The coloreds have a little boy from French Sudan. They also

dress him like a GI and have taught him to speak English. They bring him to the club when they come to town and he behaves so nicely.

The MPs have a little Arab kid they call Charlie. He's just like a big doll with black curly hair and brown eyes. He wears a pair of khaki trousers that have been cut off. You can imagine a little kid in a pair of men's trousers; it's a scream to see him with the crotch hanging almost to his knees. The MPs made him a shirt out of a striped mattress cover. He speaks English quite well because he's been with American soldiers so much of the time. I wonder if he can still speak Arabic? He stands in the door of the club and winks at me; I get so tickled at him. One day he brought a basket of eggs and said, "Mees Lady, I bring you X." I guess "X" is close enough to "eggs".

The Mascots

Just re-read this letter and it sounds disjointed, every time I get in the middle of a sentence someone starts asking questions. One boy said, "That's a good letter ain't it? I been reading it." That's the way it goes, no privacy.

May 1944

Dear Mom and Dad,
I wanted to tell you about going to Memorial Day services at the American cemetery here.

It was so lovely. The first thing that happened was that soldiers marched into the cemetery; each held a bouquet of flowers. They circled a picturesque white chapel and came to a halt beside the white crosses that marked each grave. Then five navy boys in starched whites marched in with their bouquets; two nurses in formal uniform followed them. A French band was assembled in front of the chapel; dignitaries representing the American, French and British armies gathered around the flagpole. The band played a medley of American war songs then guns were fired in salute. After the guns, at exactly the same time, each soldier leaned over and placed his bouquet on the grave next to where he stood.

Four huge wreaths were placed around the flagpole; then the Navy chaplain together with Protestant, Catholic and Jewish chaplains offered prayers for the boys buried in the cemetery. The flag was raised from half to full mast as the band played the Star-Spangled Banner.

Red poppies bloomed all over the hillside; it was an experience I'll never forget. It made me so proud to be over here sharing in all this. If only people back home could see how immaculately clean these little cemeteries are I'm sure they would feel much better about the boys they've lost.

May 1944

Dear Mom and Dad,
Have to tell you about my latest acquisition. It's a darling little
1932 green Ford convertible with red wire wheels; it has a shelter
half (actually a tent) for a convertible top. Someone painted the
name Babette, on the rear fender. Actually Babette is just a col-
lection of parts pretending to be a car. Johnny is in charge of
transportation here so I won't have to worry about the little Ford
not running well. Too bad you aren't here so I could take you for a
ride in the rumble seat. Ha ha.

Babette is right sporty for North Africa; you can't imagine how the
Arabs look at me when I come driving through town. They just stare
at me. There's one place in the road where the Arabs cross with
their sheep. I have to time it just right because if I get there
when the Arabs are crossing they stop right in front of me and
surround the car with their sheep. Then Babette dies out and I'm
stuck. When I don't show up at my destination someone knows to call
transportation and they come looking for me. But in the meantime I
have to sit in the middle of a bunch of sheep and Arabs.

Today it's pouring down rain and every GI and every stray dog is
in the club. There's an endless line of GIs yelling for doughnuts
while someone else is pounding on the piano. Several more GIs are
standing behind me with the radio blasting a play-by-play description of a football game between the Scotch and the English. Posi-
tively ripping I tell you!

A little GI with a moustache is reading this aloud to prove he can
read upside down. Someone else is on the telephone yelling, "How in
the hell do you say let's make it tomorrow in French?"

Our Arab cleaning boy and a GI from the Bronx are having a boxing
match in the only space that's open. Another GI kisses me tenderly
on both cheeks and says he's leaving for the front. The chaplain

wants me to come outside and see his amphibious jeep. Someone lost a button; Kriesel sews it on. An irate officer insists on knowing why Arabs refuse to take American gold seal
money in large dominations. Poor boy, he's been here only
two days and there's so much to learn.

American gold seal money referred to notes printed in 1934 and 1935 that were issued by the Treasurer of the United States to Federal Reserve Banks. These notes
were more than paper money; they were backed by gold bullion held by the Trea-
sury.

Wet Canadian just in on furlough and can't find a place to
sleep; somebody steps on the last ping-pong ball. Inebriat-
ed GI staggers by my desk, hesitates, then says, "Where you
from?"

I say, "Minnesota." He immediately becomes sober and

LeOna and Irene Baumann in Babette (name was written on right fender)

screams, "Migod woman, I'm from Minneapolis! I went to the University of Minnesota!"

Three GIs run in carrying another Canadian, this one knifed by Arabs. Canadian has a big tourniquet tied on his arm and looks woozy. GIs assure him he will be okay saying, "LeOna will administer first aid." Oh no, LeOna calls an ambulance, too much blood.

Two others bring in a soldier who has also been knifed by Arabs. He has a hole the size of a dollar in his head, said it felt like that knife was going clear to his toes. He was one mess of blood. I cleaned him up and called another ambulance. The doc took six stitches in his head.

Telephone rings, "We'd like 100 doughnuts for a party tonight. Could you have them ready?"

"How old are you," asks another GI? "Twenty- eight? You don't look it." "Yes she does." "No she don't."

"Got it! I took your picture Minnesota, could you get me an aspirin?"

"I'd like some v-mail, please," says another GI. French lady comes in looking for a layette. I explain this is an American club for soldiers and we don't have layettes. Newly arrived officers flood into our Enlisted Men's Club. Enlisted men complain because officers have their own club. Now I tactfully remove the officers to keep the peace.

"Where can I get a guitar? You had one in the old club. Where is it, LeOna?" " I just bought this little dog and I want you to have it". "I wanna go home, been overseas 22 months and that's too damn long!"

And so it goes, life at the Red Cross, never a dull moment!

May 1944

Dear Mom and Dad,
As I told you Irene and I eat our meals at the Officer's Club. It's located high up in the Atlas Mountains, the view from the dining room is spectacular. This city is 2,100 feet above sea level and has what's said to be the deepest ravine in the world. The bridge across the ravine was built in 1912, and it's 168 miles long.

The bridge a new pilot flew under

There are big windows all around the dining room so everyone can see the bridge and the ravine. One night we watched as some newly arrived pilot thought he'd show off and flew his plane right under the bridge. Well, that night the general happened to be eating in the club. When he saw that plane fly under the bridge he turned bright red, grabbed a pair of binoculars and shouted the plane's numbers to a major. Then, in no uncertain terms he told the major to, "Take care of it!" I bet that pilot won't ever pull a stunt like that one again!

Irene refuses to drive Babette so every night I drive the two of us up the mountain for dinner. The other night just as we started down the mountain Babette's brakes gave out. Directly ahead of us was the guardhouse

101

with a big rope stretched between it and the side of the road. The rope is the general's prized possession, it's really hard to get rope here and he had to pull a lot of strings.

When anyone drives down the mountain a guard steps from the guardhouse and says, "Stop and be identified." After people have stopped and identified themselves the guard drops the rope and the vehicle can proceed.

Well that night Babette's brakes gave out just as the GI started to step out of the guardhouse. I shouted, "Get out of the way or I'll kill ya!" He jumped back into that house so fast and just as he did Babette, Irene and I barreled right through the general's rope.

Irene was screaming we were going to be killed and I was screaming at her to be quiet so I could concentrate. Fortunately we made it to the bottom in one piece. The next night when we went back up to the club for dinner there was the general's rope, stretched back across the street, a huge knot tied in the middle!

Recently a Red Cross man asked to borrow Babette; he needed to drive somewhere out into the desert. I told him Babette wasn't very dependable but he wanted to go anyway. Of course he broke down somewhere and couldn't get back. Some GIs had to take a big truck and drive out to get him. The truck was the kind you can put a car on so they hauled both the Red Cross man and Babette back. Now they're fixing the car, they just love working on that car. It's like play for them.

Johnny wanted to write you a letter so I'll enclose it. He's so wonderful to me you can't imagine. He takes me to and from the club every night. I have a little infection in my thumb and he took me to the dispensary this morning so the doctor could lance it. He carts my laundry back and forth. That's just a small sampling of the nice things he does for me. So I hope you will write him a little letter in reply.

May 1944

Dear Mr. and Mrs. Kriesel,

LeOna is writing a letter to you so I asked if I might add a little note. Your daughter is well and happy here and doing a grand job. She is well liked by her co-workers and the pride of the enlisted men. She takes great care about the appearance of her club keeping it full of cut flowers and, "neat as wax."

I have known your daughter now for several months and can say I have never met a person so fine. I shall be ever so proud to take her to my home and present her to my parents and friends. She has spoken of you often and I shall be very happy to meet you when we get back.

We have taken several trips together in this locality and have one more pending. LeOna will undoubtedly tell you about it in another letter. We do have such a grand time together.

I will always take good care of her for you.

Sincerely,

John Cox

Road trip without guard rails and inner tubes on seats

May 1944

Dear Mom and Dad,
John and I just returned from our little trip. We really had a wonderful time. Started out Friday morning in a big command car that's
now used as an army touring car. It's mounted on a truck chassis
and rides like a lumber wagon, everything rattles! Someone gave us
the wrong directions so we chugged along over a goat trail through
the mountains. Was it ever rough! After about three hours we ran
into some Arabs who had about fifteen adult camels and lots baby
camels in tow. John said, "We really are in the wilderness. There
couldn't be much of a resort hotel in THIS area."

We weren't sure whether to turn around or not so we continued in
hopes there might be something out there. Finally we found it and
could hardly believe our eyes. Out there in the middle of nowhere
was an absolutely beautiful hotel. The architecture was French and
it was sort of a tan stucco color. It had a lovely tiled patio,
iron tables, benches and huge pots full of the biggest geraniums
I've ever seen. The hotel was "L" shaped and in the center was a
big garden filled with palm, lemon and orange trees, and roses of
every description. Hot mineral springs bubbled out from the ground.

We had no sooner registered for our rooms than John ran into a tailor he knows and guess what? The tailor's wife is the hotel manager's cousin.

The dining room looked like any hotel dining room in the States
except it was full of rich-looking French people. John asked the
waiter if he'd bring the water we put into the hotel refrigera-
tor. We had also put two bottles of Coca Cola in there. Well pretty
soon here comes the waiter; wearing his white jacket, walking very
stately and balancing a tray on the palm of his hand, his arm above
his head. On the tray were our two bottles of coke and John's old
beaten-up canteen. We started laughing and I think everyone in the
place was amused. I was so ashamed of that old canteen.

We started nibbling away at dinner consisting of an egg omelet filled with green peppers, some ground-up spinach and something else that neither of us could identify. Pretty soon the tailor's wife passed over a dish of couscous for us. One look at that ground-up concoction with big brown things in it shaped like beans and two pieces of chicken and I said, "I CAN'T eat it. I CAN'T." John said we just had to or we would offend the tailor and his wife.

Then the lady at the next table waltzed over with an artichoke. Having never seen an artichoke before I knew it was impossible for me to eat something like that so John volunteered to get rid of some of it provided I would "take on" the couscous. We began to realize it was customary to share any delicacy one brought into the dining room. Since we had a dish of peaches I had taken from the club we got into the spirit of things and passed the peaches. We offered some to an elderly man with a goatee. He wore a long black dress so John thought he was a Jewish rabbi. Well, it turned out he was a Catholic priest. He was so pleased to have peaches he insisted on saying mass for John the next morning. Said he would also say a prayer for John's parents and for you because we had been so thoughtful.

When we finished eating the tailor's wife invited us for coffee. Seems that when everyone finishes eating they gather on the patio to visit. It was all very clubby. We sat down at a table on the patio and two women came out with the blackest coffee I've ever seen in little demitasse cups. John visited with the men while I did my best with "pigeon" French and some English to show the women I was having a nice time.

The next morning I was awakened by a knock at the door. Here was a maid with a pot of that black, black coffee and two pieces of toast. John yelled in my door saying the priest had sent for him so he was going to mass.

After mass he picked me up and we went to the hotel manager's apartment for an aperitif. The tailor was waiting for us and took us to a spot under a big tree. Well, if that didn't look like something from the Gay Nineties I don't know what did. A fat man with a handlebar moustache and a white cloth for an apron was serving wine. On the table were dishes of hard-boiled eggs, celery hearts, pickled string beans and olives. Everyone from the hotel seemed to be there laughing, eating and drinking. It was really a new experience for us to see something like that. Afterward we all went to the dining room to struggle through yet another meal.

The manager's son gave me a beautiful bouquet of roses and the manager gave John a bottle of wine he said he dug out of a cave. His wife gave us a basketful of huge lemons. We left and drove like crazy to get back before the dining room closed; we were both so hungry for some plain GI food. We surely had a wonderful time though. It seemed good to get off somewhere and see civilians. A person gets tired of seeing uniforms all the time.

There's a piano recital tonight given by a well-known concert pianist in Europe. She's giving the recital at the home of a French boy I know; he's invited Irene and me.

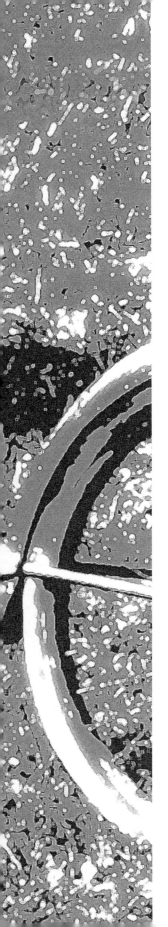
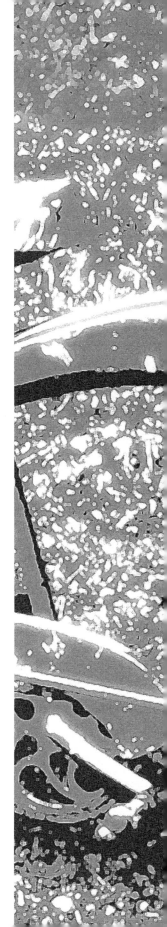

May 1944

Dear Mom and Dad,

Johnny, the Catholic chaplain and I
took a bicycle trip last week. We followed a little creek through the mountains; it was so pretty with all the
flowers in bloom. There were flowers of
all colors: yellow, orange, white, or-
chid, red and blue, plus the blooming
pecan trees.

I expect to be transferred to another
club any day now. I'm just waiting for
travel orders, so it shouldn't be long.
As I understand it censorship is much
stricter where I'll be located. Thought
that would be important to mention in
case my letters seem very different.
Rather hate to leave this place it's
been so pleasant. The French lady and
her daughters have been wonderful; they
don't want me to leave.

I'm writing to tell you about the plans
John and I are making. We know both you
and John's parents would prefer to have
us married at home and we would too.
However, it will be a long time before
either of us gets back so we've decided
to go ahead and get married here.

John is getting the papers filled out
now and will send them in for approval.
There's a lot of red tape involved so
it will be about three months before we
find out whether or not the army ap-

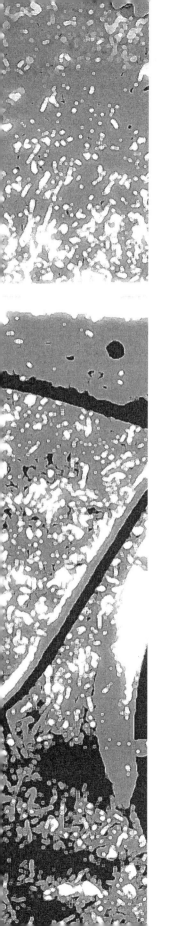
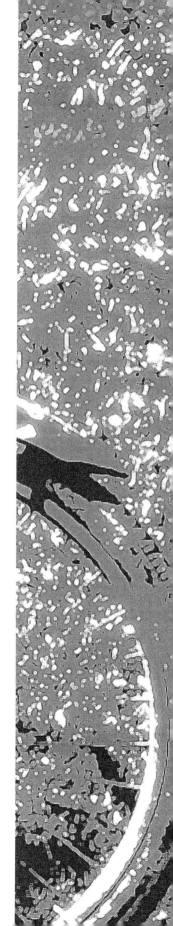

proves our request. And I have to get permission from the Red Cross. We'd like to get married next August or September. I only hope you won't be too disappointed. You know I don't like going against your wishes but I love John very much. He isn't just a passing fancy; we're both old enough to know what we want.

I will try to come home as soon as possible after the wedding. I'd like to spend some time with you while I wait for John to get back. Neither of us wants to start a family until we have a home, so you see we've considered everything. We've discussed religion, what we expect of each other after we're married, what kind of a home we want and everything else.

John is writing you a letter telling you he wants to marry me. He wants you to like him just as much as I want his parents to like me. I'm praying that you will change your minds and tell us you approve. John has already inquired and can get permission for us to have a church wedding even though I'm not Catholic.

I'd like to have you announce my engagement so people can't say you didn't know anything about it. Will you do that? Please don't worry unnecessarily, will you?

June 1944

Dear Mom and Dad,
In this letter I want to tell you some more about the Arabs before
I transfer to another country. This time I'll tell you about the
busses they have that run from one city to another. They're just a
scream. There's one model that's so huge it compares with our Grey-
hounds, but in size only.

The buses are usually dirty blue and have a contraption fastened
onto the back that holds two tanks. The tanks look like our hot water tanks but they are used to burn either wood or coal. That gen-
erates power for the bus but makes it eject huge clouds of black
smoke. The buses don't run very well they usually just snort along,
stopping now and then. Honestly, I don't see how they make it from
one place to another. There's often an Arab lying on the front
fender holding a wire that's attached to the motor. The front hood
is invariably folded back.

Talk about people being packed inside! There are so many heads in
the bus you wonder where they park their fannies. It's quite a
sight. Men wrap their heads in turbans. Women have their heads covered with black cloth; white veils extend from just under their
eyes all the way to their chins. All you see of the women are their
eyes.

Luggage is carried on top of the bus and it's not uncommon to see
about fifteen more Arabs curled up around the luggage. I've even
seen them hanging onto the ladder in back of the bus.

Some buses are very small and look homemade. They have wooden bodies placed on any kind of a chassis. A door in the back is the only
way in or out and there are wooden slats along the side. The other
noon we were riding to the hotel in an open jeep, the wind blowing
like crazy. One of those homemade looking buses was in front of us.
All of a sudden the wind got hold of some Arab's turban and that
thing unwound like a snake. Yards and yards of material went flying
through the air and blew right into our jeep! Golly we did laugh.

Bugs are common around here; the Arabs take them in stride. We see Arab men sitting in the sun pulling bugs from their clothing and putting them on the ground. Someone said it's against their religion to kill the bugs, or at least to kill them in daylight. Anyway, the movie theaters here sell tickets in advance and all seats are reserved. There's a captain who buys five seats whenever he goes to the movie. Then he sits in the center with two empty seats on either side of him to make sure there isn't any Arab within bug-jumping distance of him. Personally I won't even go to the public theaters. You know how scared I am of a "louse."

Irene served ice cream today in the snack bar. She made the mix with canned milk, chocolate and powdered eggs. It was very good considering everything. Anyway, the club was humming like a bee-hive; five minutes after the snack bar opened you could hear a pin drop. Every GI in here was eating ice cream and the happy looks on their faces made it worth the effort. They were like a bunch of little kids.

You asked if we serve beer in the club. No, we don't. No liquor of any sort is allowed in a Red Cross club or at any dance sponsored by the Red Cross. That's because the public supports Red Cross and we would be criticized for allowing alcohol. In fact, MPs keep drunks from even hanging around the club.

June 1944

Dear Mom and Dad,
The Red Cross director told me I could have a few days off to rest before I'm transferred. John got two-and-a-half days leave so he, Ruby (a Red Cross Girl from Montana) and I went to a beautiful resort hotel on the Mediterranean. We packed food, bathing suits, shorts and uniforms. Then crammed ourselves and our luggage into an open jeep. Things like that don't matter over here. Back home I wouldn't have imagined riding in a jeep from Ortonville to Minneapolis packed in the way we were.

John had thoughtfully placed partially inflated inner tubes inside the cushions to make our seats a little softer. He didn't think about how bumpy the roads are in North Africa. The entire way Ruby and I hung on for dear life for fear we'd bounce right out of the jeep.

The trip was simply beautiful; we drove through the mountains, winding to the top and back down again. There were ferns and beautiful flowers everywhere. At one point we drove through a beautiful canyon that I'll never forget. Once we got out of the mountains the "highway" ran alongside of the Mediterranean. There were dark red and pink rhododendrons everywhere.

The big white stucco hotel was right on the beach; each room had a little balcony. The dining room had ceiling to floor windows. The side that faced the sea was all glass. Outside was a huge patio with tables and wicker chairs. After settling into our rooms we donned shorts and shirts and went to the beach. All we wanted to do was swim, wade, pick up shells, lie in the sun and relax. It was wonderful after having been around the GIs all these months.

The food was very good. I tasted the butter and said, "Gee, THIS is really good butter. This tastes like Minnesota butter." Well, John and Ruby razzed me about that until we found the paper the butter was packed in and guess what it said? "Land O Lakes, Minneapolis, Minnesota." So all the time we were there John and Ruby would kid me about having GOOD butter, MINNESOTA butter. NO kidding, you can tell it easily. It's much more yellow than the butter we get from the East coast and it has a different flavor altogether.

On the way home we saw Arabs cutting their hay and grain. Men and women worked side-by-side cutting the crops with little sickles; they looked so colorful out in the field. The women had their heads wrapped in brightly colored red, yellow, purple and blue cloth. Men, women and children were all working and all were barefoot.

Once the Arabs had gathered bunches of grain and bundled them the men stacked them on the heads of the women and children! I don't see how those women, and certainly the children, could even walk. They looked like straw piles with bare feet. The men didn't tax themselves they tied their bundles onto the backs of donkeys. The poor little donkeys would be lucky if their ears were sticking out.

Remember when I wrote about the locusts? Well the little ones have hatched now and the highways are covered with them. Arabs were sweeping them from the roads with tree branches; when they got a big pile of locusts they either burned them or motioned for us to drive over them with our jeeps. We must've killed thousands of locusts.

This morning we saw Arab women going after water, each woman had a huge pottery jug on her head. The women who were going to market were all dolled up in white robes and veils. They straddled beaten-up old horses and sat on something that looked like feedbags covered with bright red and yellow striped blankets. Baskets usually hung from the horse's rear ends. When a man is riding the horse the woman sits behind him with her feet in the baskets. More often the man rides and the woman walks. I get a big kick out of these sights.

Well let's see, what else did I want to tell you in this letter? Oh yes, I want to tell you about the cloth ears the Arabs made for their mules and old, sway-backed horses. The idea is to protect the animals from having flies in their ears. Well, the other day I saw a crude looking cart with a mule and two donkeys hitched to it. The mule had blue ears with white flowers on it. One donkey had yellow ears with little blue flowers and the other had pink ears with green flowers. I just stood on the street corner and laughed. It was all so colorful and their ears were so big!

John and I drove through the Arab district the other day just as a group of Arabs were preparing to pray. They took off their shoes and washed their feet in a spring. One by one they knelt on the ground and bent over from the hips. Then they start going slowly up and down, it looked like they were kissing the ground.

Yesterday I had my teeth fixed. This dentist's "office" was a little higher class than the last. This one had a partially screened tent and a drill with a motor! Of course once the dentist got my mouth all tied up and packed full of cotton, the motor wouldn't start. Had to wait until some enterprising GI discovered the trouble and fixed it. The army doesn't believe in Novocain and I think

I twisted around that drill a few times. The stool I had to sit on didn't have anything to put your feet on so I couldn't even brace myself.

After that ordeal I went to the dispensary and asked to have my Typhoid and Typhus booster shots. As the GIs prepared the serum a major yelled, "Get me the spray!" The spray was actually some kind of liquid anesthetic. All of a sudden there was bedlam in the dispensary as GIs ran around with bottles of this stuff and squirted the huge flies, freezing them right in their tracks. When all the flies were dead, I got my shots.

John on motor bike in North Africa

June 1944

Dear Mom and Dad,
I'm still here in Africa but expect to leave very soon. Have been
so busy since Irene left and I've been operating the club alone.
A new girl came in and I had just gotten her settled when two more
new girls arrived.

Can't you just picture me trying to write the monthly reports? Com-
piling all the figures on what we've used from the storeroom, taking inventory, balancing books, posting financial statements and
on and on, all while these new girls talked nonstop and asked questions, "Where can I get my hair done? What kind of a program could
we have? Why don't you have movies? Where can we get a projec-
tor? How much are our meals? Where do you buy supplies? Where's the
APO?" One girl is a typical old maid. She ran a dormitory at the
University of Michigan and I bet she was a terror, seems the type.
Anyway what with packing and all I think you'll understand why I
haven't written for over a week. Those new girls have driven me almost crazy.

A Red Cross man who runs a little club up the line was in today and
told me a funny story. He said some boy stuck his head in the office and said, "Sir, may I come in like this?" The Red Cross man
said of course he could come in and with that seven GIs came into
the man's office. They were all wearing bathing trunks and were
soaking wet. Seems they had run out of cigarettes while their lib-
erty ship was anchored off the coast and they needed to get to the
Red Cross club to get some more. There was a $25 fine for anyone
caught rowing a lifeboat to shore so these GIs swam! The man telling me the story was laughing so hard he was shaking. Said he'd had
boys hitch rides on every kind of conveyance to get to his club but
this was the first time he'd ever had anyone swim. Their boat was
moored quite a distance from shore.

That's the "can do" American spirit for you!

June 1944

Dear Mom and Dad,

The box of music came, thanks a lot. We certainly use it; our sheet music is just about worn out. The boys like to sing morning, noon and night. You can't imagine how the boys love to get around a piano and sing.

You asked about Johnny's religion. Yes, he's Catholic. However, I'm sure that won't make any difference to either one of us. We've talked it all over very sensibly with both chaplains and see no reason why it won't work out. Johnny graduated from a Methodist university. He said his parents didn't care what my religion was as long as I came from a good family and was a nice girl.

He's crazy about sports, likes to swim, bicycle, skate and picnic, just as I do. My landlady and her daughters just love him. They're always inviting us in for cake or custard after I finish work in the evening. He treats them very nicely, always fixing things for them. Don't feel that I am being hasty; I'm old enough to know what I want and to use good judgment. If we do get married over here it will be because we know where Johnny will be located and what kind of job he will have. As a married couple we'll be able to save more money. Johnny's salary would be greatly increased to cover maintenance for me as his dependent.

Honestly, I get so tired of people reading over my shoulder when I am typing a letter. I just told someone to quit reading this. It's very hot out today; we're having a "Sirocco," or in other words, a good old South Dakota dirt storm.

The locust moved in today, they're so thick and big they look like birds swarming everywhere. The locust are about two inches long with a wingspan of about five inches. They look like grasshoppers; Arabs are out batting them with sticks. The boys tell me the Arabs bake and string them. They wear the baked locust around their necks and sell them on the street.

We started taking Malaria pills now. They are so bitter and hard to take but if we get malaria they're supposed to help us not to get it so badly. As long as that's the case, I guess I can swallow anything. Starting the fifteenth of this month we had to put a framework over our bed and cover it with army-issue mosquito netting. It certainly seems funny, like sleeping in a little tent.

A Sirocco is a hot dust-laden wind from the Libyan deserts that blows with hurricane force onto the northern Mediterranean coast.

June 1944

Dear Mr. and Mrs. Kriesel,

Just a brief note to inform you that mail from LeOna may be slow for a short time. Undoubtedly you have heard that she was leaving this fair country of North Africa for sunny Italy. Which is really quite a joke as every time that I have been over there it poured down rain. Anyway, this morning I bade her farewell at the airport and she was off in a flash.

She is a picture of health after having spent several days resting up before taking on new duties. She was quite tired and the well-deserved rest came just in time. Her tan is coming along swell. She is still very active and enjoying her work.

I'm already quite lonesome since she left but I hope to get up to see her shortly. We'll take a "Cook's Tour" of one of the large towns there. Censorship regulations preclude any further information but we'll save all the pictures and things we collect to really have a good old-fashioned bull session when we're all together.

The other day we went for a picnic in a picturesque part of the city. We borrowed a camera and got some beautiful pictures. They should prove to be a good evening's entertainment. LeOna and I are in about every scene. No, we are not camera-shy!

She is one fine girl and I love her very much.

My sincere best wishes,

John Cox

THE EUROPEAN THEATRE
1944

Landing on Normany Beach, France, June 6, 1944
Chief Photographer's Mate (CPHOM) Robert F. Sargent, U.S. Coast Guard

In early January 1944, Allied Forces broke through the German line and advanced to Cassino. The Allies planned to engage the German Tenth Army along the Gustav Line and when it was secured an amphibious landing at Anzio would follow. The assault on the Gustav Line began January 17th, with minor success. On January 22nd, General Lucas' VI Corps successfully landed at Anzio and faced a strong German counterattack. After 2 1/2 months of fighting the Allied assault was stalled both at Cassino and Anzio.

May 11, 1944, Allied Forces launched a coordinated attack to penetrate the Gustav Line at Cassino and break out of the Anzio beachhead. The attack around Cassino stalled but French and American forces along the Mediterranean coast broke through and advanced toward Anzio. Meanwhile the reinforced VI Corp, now under the command of General Truscott, advanced north toward Rome. However a stout German defense near the Alban Hills, south of Rome, held off the Allied offensive long enough for the trapped German Tenth Army to escape. Allied forces pursued the retreating Nazis and by mid-June had pushed the German defenses back to a line about half way between Rome and Florence.

June 4, 1944, elements of General Mark Clark's 5th Army entered central Rome; German forces withdrew to the north. In his radio broadcast that night President Franklin D. Roosevelt proclaimed, "One up. Two to go," referring to the surrender of the first of three Axis capitals.

Rome celebrated and huge crowds gathered in the streets; they cheered, waved and threw flowers at the Allies. Fortunately Rome was left relatively undamaged by war. That night Pope Pius XII appeared at the balcony of St. Peter's and told thousands below, "In recent days we trembled for the fate of the city. Today we rejoice because, thanks to the joint goodwill of both sides, Rome has been saved from the horrors of war."

The following morning, June 6th, was D-Day, the Allied invasion of Normandy. Meanwhile on the Eastern Front, German advances into Russia had peaked in November 1942. Nazis then controlled about 1/3 of Russia, from Leningrad on the Gulf of Finland, to Stalingrad on the north, and south to the Caucasus Mountains. By June 1944, the Russian Army had regained the Motherland and pushed German forces into Poland and Rumania.

Hitler's dream of the Third Reich was rapidly collapsing.

LEONA REMEMBERS

B-24 Liberator Bomber, US Airforce Image Library of Congress circa 1945

I was transferred to Rome, Italy on June 23, 1944, shortly after Rome fell, **began LeOna in a speech delivered at Raymond Walters College in Cincinnati, Ohio.**

When I received transfer orders the date stipulated for me to leave was the same day the gang planned to give me a big farewell party. I couldn't miss that so John asked two of his pilot friends from the XII Air Force & Training Command Headquarters in Constantine, Major

Colonel John R. "Killer" Kane commanded the 98th Bomb Group, known as the "Pyramiders." During his time in North Africa Colonel Kane flew 43 combat missions.

He was awarded the Medal of Honor on August 9, 1943, for bravery during Operation Tidal Wave, the most highly decorated military mission in U.S. history. The mission was to destroy the largest of the Nazi-held oil refineries at Ploesti, 30 miles north of Bucharest, Romania. Colonel Kane's Medal of Honor citation reads in part, "By his gallant courage, brilliant leadership, and superior flying skill, he and the formation under his command successfully attacked this vast refinery so essential to our enemies' war effort."

Hutton and Colonel "Killer" Kane, if they could fly me to Rome the day after the party. That way I could still make my report date in Rome.

The pilots said they couldn't get me all the way to Rome but they could get me to Naples since they had orders to fly to Naples the day of the party and they planned to make an unscheduled landing to pick up their girlfriends, nurses in a field hospital. They'd have to get the girls back the next day and said I could go too.

The only catch was the pilots didn't have orders to take the B-24 out again the next day but they had a plan. They were going to make sure the general got drunk at the party and then give him fake orders to sign allowing them to take the plane out for a test run. The plan worked. Major Hutton and Colonel Kane knew they had to get to Naples and back before the general sobered up, found out the plane was gone, and remembered what had happened. John was told to have me at the airport by 5:00 a.m. The 600-mile flight to Naples took 2 hours and 13 minutes in the bomber. If all went as planned the pilots could get to Naples and back before 10:00 in the morning.

When we arrived at the airport the pilots were already in the cockpit, the nurses were up front in the nose. I had to sit in the back with my legs wrapped around the gun mount! Looking up through the turret all I could see was the sky. Off we went; I was so claustrophobic I could hardly stand it.

All of a sudden, bumpty, bump, bump, we landed on something that surely didn't feel like a runway. When we came to a stop I heard the pilots talking outside the plane so I began beating on the side to get their attention. Major Kane opened the door and said, "What's with you back here? Just hang tight. We're dropping the girls off and then going right on to Naples."

LeOna continued, "Well," I said "I don't like it back here." To which Colonel Kane asked, "Why not?" I said, "Suppose something happened, how would I get out?" He countered by saying, "So where would you go?"

The two pilots must have felt a little sorry for me so they said I could come up front with them but I'd have to stand in the Plexiglas nose. So there I was, completely surrounded by the plane's Plexiglas nose. Over Naples I saw Kane and Hutton give each other a little nudge and with that they put the B-24 into a dive. Straight down we went, 107-miles an hour into Naples! I felt like a bird watching the runway coming straight up at me. At the last minute they pulled out of the dive and made a neat landing. As soon as we were on the ground they shouted for me to jump out and run as fast as I could, they didn't want to account for me in flight operations. I was so scared I was shaking; when I got to the Red Cross shack all I could say was, "Give me coffee!"

From Naples I had to find my own transportation to Rome. There was another Red Cross girl at the airport who was also headed to Rome so we agreed to go together. When we checked around we found the only thing going was a convoy of tanks; we asked the commanding officer if we could join them. He told us to get a car and fall in line with the tanks, which we did. He cautioned us to stay within the white tape that stretched endlessly on both sides of the road. That's as far as the road had been cleared of land mines. Tanks don't move very fast and it was a long way from Naples to Rome so I asked the commander about going to the bathroom. He said we'd have to squat next to the car!

It took us all day and into the evening to get to Rome because we had to stop for hours in Casino to let tanks from the north pass as they returned to Naples. I'll never forget the sight of Casino as long as I live. It was horrible, horrible, horrible; now I realize what they mean by "no man's land!" Piles of rubble from bombed buildings covered the landscape, not a thing was left standing. All the trees had been turned into charred stumps, no more than three to five feet tall. Everywhere there were signs reading, Mines, Booby Traps, Mines cleared 20 feet. Seeing this I couldn't help but think of the war stories the men in town used to tell when we were kids.

Saw some fancy foxholes, wonderful examples of Yankee ingenuity.

Italy
June 1944

Dear Mom and Dad,
Italy is a wonderful place compared to North Africa. I didn't realize how much I've missed being in a city until I got back to a city. Gosh it's wonderful.

I ran into a major I knew today, he's going back to the States and said he'd mail this letter for me when he got there. Be sure to let me know you got it. Your letters to me aren't censored so you don't have to be afraid to write anything. You can ask me questions and I can reply the best I can. Perhaps you have already guessed that I'm in Rome. I can confirm it only because this letter is going to be mailed in the States and won't go through the censors.

I'm living in a hotel that's only a year old. The floor is made of inlaid wooden squares. I have twin beds with a table between them. The phone on the table allows me to push a red button that flashes, "Do not disturb" outside my door. If I push the green button an Italian word meaning "Enter" goes on. The bathroom is all green tiles and has modern fixtures. There's a shower in the tub and oh yes, there's indirect lighting above the tub. That's so the light won't shine in your eyes dearie. I have beautiful red rugs in the bedroom and lots of closet space. There are even glass drawers in one section. Dear me, such luxury.

In the dining room meals are served on Swedish modern tables with upholstered chairs. The tables are set with beautiful white and blue china with gold borders. Every day there are fresh flowers and candles on the tables. The waiters wear tuxedo trousers with white jackets in the morning and at noon; at night they wear tails. I haven't been able to eat or sleep well because everything's much too fancy. After all I've been eating from tin pie plates and drinking out of cut-off bottles for the last year. A maid does our laundry, presses our clothes and polishes our shoes. Nope, it just can't last. I'm skeptical.

June 1944

Dear Mom and Dad,
Isn't the news about the invasion good? I actually saw the planes
flying over on the way to that big event. It was quite a thrill and
it was also really scary. Everyone expected the worst.

When men from a tank battalion returned I listened as they said,
with tears in their eyes, "We're lucky, we made it through this
one. They said we were finished but now we're being told we have to
go back to the front again."

Operation OVERLORD, the invasion of Normandy, is considered the decisive battle of World War II. It took place in June 1944. Prior to the invasion of Normandy the German Army occupied France and the Low Countries, Belgium, the Netherlands and Luxembourg. This gave the Nazis valuable access to Western Europe's raw materials and industrial capacity.

After the invasion of Normandy and the expansion of the initial beachheads, Allied armies took the offensive. The invasion of Normandy, Operation OVERLORD, hit the German army hard in every respect. It landed psychological and physical blows from which they never recovered and turned the tide of World War II.

We've learned the tank battalion is scheduled for another invasion,
this time in southern France. The men cried as they showed me pictures of their families. Then I cried.

The Allied invasion of southern France took place later in the summer of 1944. Code named ANVIL and DRAGOON, the invasion of southern France was originally planned to coincide with the invasion of Normandy. However it took place five weeks later. The outcome was the capture of Toulon and Marseilles and access to Lyon and Dijon in the Rhone River valley. This gave armies based in Normandy the opportunity to advance even farther east toward Germany.

July 1944

Dear Mom and Dad,
Today, I start work with the Assistant Program Director in a beautiful club. She's in charge of entertainment and I'm supposed to help her. Of course that's what I love to do so I'm really happy. We're working on a big dance for the Fourth of July.

The club is located in a lovely park with trees everywhere; it looks like a big outdoor beer garden. There's a tile patio with a fountain; around the fountain are umbrella tables and chairs. In the back there's an outdoor snack bar and in the center there's a big stage with a white band shell. That's where we'll have stage shows and plays.

The building is very pretty; it has balconies galore. There's a big room where the boys can read and write letters. Another room has billiard and ping-pong tables, plus a table for wrapping packages.

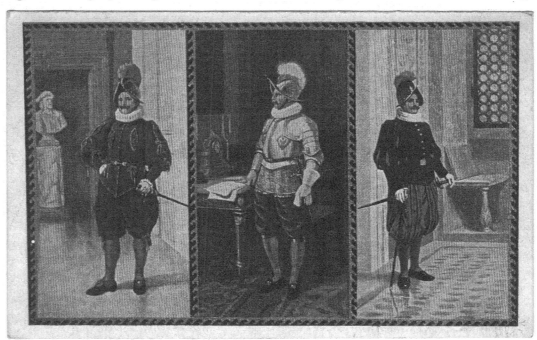

Above and Right: Postcards from LeOna's visits to the Vatican

There's a room with an electric radio, phonograph and grand piano.
Actually, the whole thing looks like something out of the movies.

Hope I can stay here permanently however that might not be possible. I may have to move on and open a small club somewhere else.

Weighed myself yesterday and I've gained 17 pounds! No wonder I had to let out my uniforms. Guess it's a good thing I ate so well in Africa because we don't have food like that here. Must be harder to get in Italy.

KING VICTOR EMMANUE
MONUMENT. ROME

July 1944

Dear Mom and Dad,
I want to give you an idea what it's like here in this club. We entertain between 16,000 and 17,000 men per day. From the time we open until the time we close, we make coffee. Every forty minutes we make 30 gallons of coffee in 30-gallon garbage cans that sit on seven little camp stoves. We constantly give out coffee, donuts and sandwiches.

Pope Pius XII

We also take the boys on outings and plan entertainment for them. I wanted to take the boys into town to see Pope Pius XII offer prayers in the Sistine Chapel. In order for us to get there the boys from the railway battalion made us an old bus put together from spare parts. Italian guides were supposed to go with us as interpreters, but when I asked, none were willing to go. They said seeing the Pope was a very solemn occasion in Italy and they didn't want to chance any inappropriate behavior on the part of the GIs. I promised nothing would happen and said the boys would be fine, I told them I was absolutely sure of it. On my word the Italians relented and agreed to accompany us. We all climbed onto the old bus and headed for Rome. When we got into the Sistine Chapel we found ourselves standing right along the path where Pope Pius XII would walk. Wouldn't you know it, just as the Pope was passing us a little GI who was down on his knees yelled, "Hey Pope, wait a moment, I wanna take your picture."

That finished us with the Italian guides. The next time I wanted to take GIs to Rome Irene and I had to take them by ourselves, which we did. This time as we entered the Sistine Chapel thousands of people were already there, mostly soldiers. Irene and I were the only women. I smiled at one of the Swiss Guards because I thought he looked so cute. His uniform was made of yellow, red and blue striped material with puffy sleeves and billowing pantaloons. On his feet were big-buckled black shoes and on his head was a helmet with crimson plumes. When he saw me smile at him he came over and took me by the arm. I thought he was going to throw me out; I told him I hadn't done anything wrong. When he realized what I was thinking he let go of my arm and motioned for me to follow him. With that he walked me right in front of the Pope's raised platform.

When Pope Pius XII emerged he walked directly to where I was standing. When he finished offering prayers in three languages he looked straight down at me and asked who I was and where I was from. I told him I was a Red Cross girl from Minnesota. To which the Pope replied that he had visited St. Paul and Minneapolis when he was a Cardinal and liked the twin cities very much. He said the people were so friendly.

I told him I knew about his visit because I was a student at the University of Minnesota at the time; I said everyone there loved him. With that the Pope lowered his hand to me. I had no idea what he was doing and the minute I hesitated the crowd swelled and practically crushed me. Later I found out he was offering his ring for me to kiss but not being Catholic I didn't know that was a big honor.

July 1944

Dear Mom and Dad,
Hope I get some mail from you pretty soon. When I don't hear from
you it seems you're so far away.

Last night I dreamed about you again. In my dream I got off the
train and you were there to meet me. When we got home I ran up-
stairs to the kitchen and opened the icebox; it was full of ber-
ries, fresh vegetables and bottles of milk. I was so happy I cried.
I grabbed the milk and told you I hadn't tasted milk since the 17th
of November 1943. I woke up just as I was about to drink it. Oh
yes, there was a big plate of your chocolate cupcakes in the icebox
Mom. That was a wonderful dream.

I love my work in this big club. I work with the sweetest girl from
St. Louis and two lovely women who manage the club's music room.
Both music room ladies volunteered to work with us and they're wonderful. One lady is a Russian actress and married to an Italian
movie producer. The other girl was brought up in England. She's the
daughter of a diplomat and married to an Italian newspaper corre-
spondent. They've lived in Paris, Berlin and lots of other places
throughout Europe.

We have any number of countesses, baronesses and other royals working here and at the officer's club. The Fascists took all their
money and now they don't have enough food to eat so they work for
us to earn money. It seems the better class of people here are not
Fascists, they love the Americans and treat us wonderfully. One of
the countesses baked a big birthday cake, complete with candles,
for a GI who'd been overseas for 30 months. He was so tickled he
cried. They open their homes to the soldiers and to us.

One lady told me everyone marvels at how kind American soldiers
are to children. The GIs are always "borrowing" kids from ladies
sitting in the park. They love to bring them to the club for ice
cream. The boys will stand in line for 45 minutes to get a dish
of ice cream and then give it to some little kid. The other night
two boys were on their way downtown and saw a little girl crying her heart out. She said her mother had scolded her because she

couldn't get her arithmetic right. The GIs brought her to the club and helped her with the arithmetic problems. When she finished they gave her ice cream and let her play the piano. Think every boy in here took turns holding her on his lap. Pretty soon a frantic mother came running in looking for her little girl. When they left one of the boys said, "Jeez! That's the best time I've ever had overseas. Wasn't she cute?"

Last night I saw an Italian man stop his bicycle, untie a little curly-haired baby and hand her to a big GI. The GI carried her down the street and I thought the boy would love that baby to death. My friend, Mrs. Govoni, said, "I can't get over how big-hearted the Americans are. Everyone is impressed with your kindness and how much the soldiers love children."

Drawing from a Red Cross hand out

I'm living in a beautiful new hotel, can have a hot bath every morning! Our food isn't too good, mostly "C" rations, but it's surprising what they do with it. Since I gained 17 pounds in Africa it'll be just as well if I don't eat so much and lose some weight.

Had my hair styled by a stylist from Paris named Tullio. Thanks to almost a year in North Africa I could actually carry on quite a conversation with him in French. In Paris Tullio designed clothes for Italian, French and Russian movie stars; then he'd style their hair to go with his costumes. I asked if he'd like to design my wedding dress and he was thrilled to death. He said it would be better if his friend Fernanda Gattinoni designed my dress, underwear and even my shoes! He would design my hairstyle and makeup.

Fernanda Gattinoni began her fashion career at the Molineaux atelier in London. From there she worked in the Ventura fashion house in Milan. In 1934, Ventura opened an office in Rome and name Gattinoni design director.

She worked in Rome throughout World War II and eventually founded her own atelier on the Via Marche in 1945. Gattinoni became famous for her sumptuous wedding gowns. Her designs featured lavish hand embroidery (she employed 25 embroiderers) and long veils.

When the sister of Reza Shah Pahlavi, ruler of what was then Persia, was married, Gattinoni designed the gown.

In 1950, she became even more of an international sensation with clients that included Princess Margaret, Audrey Hepburn, Ingrid Bergman, Eva Peron, Gina Lollobrigida, Angie Dickinson, Kim Novak and Anna Magnani. She designed Audrey Hepburn's costumes for the movie War and Peace, which earned her an Oscar nomination in 1956.

Tullio wants to get into Vogue magazine. I told him about my friend from training, Bettina Wilson, the former society editor of Vogue. Coincidentally Bettina is here in Rome and works at the same hotel where the beauty shop is located. Said I'd introduce him to Bettina and better yet I'd invite her to the wedding so she could see exactly what he could do. He just gasped and said, "Mademoiselle, I'll make you the loveliest bride in the entire world!"

I told him he will get good publicity because I'll be sure people know the dress is an original by Gattinoni and hair by Tullio. He really got excited then and said he'll start giving me facials now so my skin will be flawless. He's going to restyle my hair for the veil Gattinoni is planning. The morning of the wedding Tullio insists on doing my makeup, fixing my hair and putting on the final touches. I'm so excited; wish you could be here for it. Think it'll be really swell.

Mrs. Govoni wants to help me with all the plans. I told you about her, she's the wife of an Italian diplomat. Well, she wants us to be married in the most beautiful church in Rome. I said, "But I'm not Catholic." She said, "It makes no difference. My husband will insist upon you being allowed to be married there."

John wrote that our papers have arrived at Headquarters; that means we should be able to get married the latter part of August or September. The way it looks, he's going to be stationed near here. We're certainly hoping it'll work out that way. Please don't be disappointed about our decision not to wait until after the war to be married. You shouldn't worry that I might change my mind. I won't.

John's so disappointed you never acknowledged his letter. His father wrote me a lovely letter. I hope you'll write him because he looks for a letter from you every day. When I left Africa I couldn't write for a while. I know John wrote you a note the day I left. He thought you'd worry if you didn't hear from me. That's how thoughtful he is. I really hope you'll write to him.

Goodwin Home, Haverhill, Massachusetts

Haverhill, Massachusetts
July 1944

Dear LeOna,
I hardly know how to start a letter to a young lady after so many years of writing to the boys. It was always the same town gossip and sports events so it was easy writing to them.

In John's last letter he told us of his coming marriage to you and we are very happy. From all he has told us we know that you both will be very happy. We will do everything we can to make it so. If we can read pictures you are tops, so we send you our congratulations and hope God will watch over you and John.

We are proud of our boys. They have always been a credit to us and we have never heard they were anything but gentlemen. Which is why they have so many friends. However, they do have their other sides. They can be balky, which is the English in them. We hope that your parents will like John.

I should have written to you before but I picked a good day. D-day here. This morning, at 4:15 a.m., sirens and ringing church bells awakened us. Here it was not a day of celebration but one of solemnity. The churches filled with people, many of whom stayed there for hours. We all pray that everyone will be home soon.

Sincerely,

Mr. and Mrs. J.V. Cox

Mode of transport typical in Rome circa 1944

July 1944

Dear Mom and Dad,

I like my work very much. Our club is beautiful and the girls are the nicest I've ever met. To make things really tops John was transferred here. He was given a wonderful assignment in the personnel section of the second-highest headquarters in this area. The commanding officer said he should get his captaincy soon and that he can go as high as major in this particular job. It's the same kind of work he was doing in North Africa, but that colonel down there seemed to approve promotions only for high-ranking officers. Some colonel John had worked with earlier gave the commanding officer here a wonderful recommendation for John. That was the reason he got this good job.

Our papers were approved so we set September 1st as the date for our wedding. Gattinoni changed her mind about how she wants to design my dress now she plans to use heavy white satin with an overlay of hand-embroidered lace. The embroidered design will be lilies of the valley. Gattinoni says it will take many girls, many days to do the work because it all has to be done by hand. It's going to be the most beautiful dress you can imagine. The veil she designed is lovely too; Tullio plans to fasten it in my hair with real flowers.

July 1944

Dear Mom and Dad,
Had a funny experience the other night. Was talking to a gang of boys at the club when someone said, "See that fellow over there? He's from Minnesota."

I replied, "Could be with that blonde hair." The boy came over and asked where I was from. When I said I was from Ortonville, he screamed, "I'm from Big Stone!" When I told him my name he said, "My cousin is married to a guy named Emmett Kriesel."

I exclaimed, "Why that's my brother!" The boys got such a kick out of it. The boy seemed so happy to run into someone from home; he's planning to ask his commanding officer for a weekend off so he can come to the club and just talk for two days. I dug out the Ortonville papers you sent, I always keep them at the club just in case I see someone from home. That boy was so thrilled to see them; all the trouble you went to sending them to me was worth it. Be sure to tell Emmett and Babe about me meeting Babe's cousin from Big Stone.

We're very busy at the club. If you can imagine, we have eight times the number of people that live in Ortonville go through our snack bar every day. They're all looking for coffee, cake and ice cream. And all they want to do is talk; talk and talk and talk. That's why I'm all pooped out at night. The boys say, "Keep on talking, sister. We don't care what you talk about. We just wanna listen to an American girl talk."

Thousands of times a day I say, "I'm from Minnesota. Town named Ortonville, southwestern part of the state, yes, I've lived in Minneapolis. No I don't know your gunner from Cass Lake, or your buddy from St. Paul, or your mother in-law from South Minneapolis. Yes, I've been overseas eight months. I was in North Africa before I came here. Yes, the Arabs are really dirty." It's always the same conversation.

They're dying to visit and the first thing they want to know is where you're from and how many months you've been overseas. That's the cue to ask the GI where he's from and how many months he's been overseas. They never say two years, it's always precisely calculated in months: 24 months, 30 months and so on. The next sentence is always, "Boy, wouldn't 'cha like to be back in the States?"

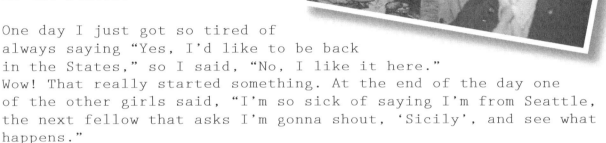

One day I just got so tired of always saying "Yes, I'd like to be back in the States," so I said, "No, I like it here." Wow! That really started something. At the end of the day one of the other girls said, "I'm so sick of saying I'm from Seattle, the next fellow that asks I'm gonna shout, 'Sicily', and see what happens."

We have lots of laughs and I wouldn't trade this experience for anything!

JOURNAL *Final*

...Y 14, 1944   Price 3 Cents in Twin City Area 5 Cents Elsewhere

Strong Allied Att Below Rome Rep

Haverhill, Massachusetts
August 1944

Dear LeOna,
We were happy to get your last letter and hope that you will keep us informed of what is going on over there with you and John. He would never go into detail about your wedding preparations. He'd never tell us about your gown and your hairdresser. You cover them all and we love it.

Don't worry about your cooking satisfying John. He has had some experience along that line so let him do some of it. Anyway you can always call on us at any time to help with anything. Mr. and Mrs. Goodwin, who are very good friends of the family, will soon write you a letter. Mrs. Goodwin has been very fond of John since his high school days as he was a pal of her son. From what we have told her about you we think you would not mind if we let her have a peek at your letter. John has written about you and they have gone all out for you as we have. We will all be glad when the both of you come home.

In our last letter to William we sent him your congratulations. You will like him; he's a fine boy (they are still boys to us). We had a wonderful time in New York and, like all parents, we were proud of our son in whites, (he's now a Navy Ensign). He did look good! In fact he looked as good as the Admiral. We met many people from different states; their feelings were the same as ours about having sons in New York. At that time of the year it is very hot. The day of graduation it was 97-degrees.

We were so glad to get on the train to come home only to find it just as hot here.

We have not been many places this summer as we have rented the beach cottage. Because of the war, workers are making so much money it just burns holes in their pockets. They are willing to pay any price for a cottage, or hotel room, at the beach. We get about the same people every year renting our cottage.

We are waiting for something to break over there then we will start having fun. One cannot have a good time with the boys so far away. Our minds are on them all the time. But we know that you will take part of that load from our minds. Judging from the letters he sends we believe you are just the lady for John. He is very much in love with you and we are thankful. We, too, have become very fond of you.

We will write again soon. If you have time, send us the news about everything.
As ever,

Mr. and Mrs. Cox

August 1944

Dear Mom and Dad,
So Dad has German prisoners working for him at the power plant?
I bet everyone out there treats them like Americans. If only I
could tell you about the atrocities the Germans have committed in
this city alone I doubt you'd ever believe me. When we get back we
can tell you some tales that will make you sick to your stomach.
There are civilians here who've lost members of their families and
they've told us dreadful things.

After dinner John and I went for a walk on a road that runs along
the sea. All of a sudden we heard a huge noise and saw great clouds
of smoke. A mine had exploded a couple of blocks from where we were
walking! That was the end of our walking around. We went to a dance
in a beautiful villa overlooking the Tyrrhenian Sea. The dance was
held on a second-floor balcony. The orchestra was playing inside so
the only light on the balcony was from the full moon. It was beautiful.

August 1944

Dear Mom and Dad,

I'm busy as can be with all the final wedding plans. Surely wish you could be here for it. An army chaplain will marry us. He got special permission for us to be married in front of the main alter of the big Catholic cathedral even though I'm not Catholic. You can't imagine what it's like being a Protestant and trying to marry a Catholic in Rome!

My dress is simply beautiful. Gattinoni changed the design again, now it's going to be an evening dress made out of white taffeta and covered with a separate, dress of silk tulle. Tiny sprays of Lilly of the Valley are being hand appliquéd onto the tulle. The back of the dress has a darling bustle and a long train. My veil, also made of tulle, goes to the floor.

The girls are having a party for me next Wednesday night. The officers are having a "bachelor" party for John. We're having such a good time and didn't expect all this attention. The Red Cross is giving us the wedding reception in the roof garden of the hotel where we live. They're having an orchestra and I'm sure it will be a lovely affair. Oh how I wish you could be here. John's colonel is sending a plane to Sicily to pick up Champagne for the reception. That's how much everyone likes John!

We'll be married at noon on September 1st. Allied Force Headquarters Public Relations Department is sending photographers to the wedding and the reception. Pictures and stories will be sent to the newspapers where John and I have lived and gone to school. The 12th Air Force and ARC photographers will also be here.

We are both getting 15-day leaves and will have our honeymoon at big resort hotel on the Isle of Capri. John has the address of a man who rents sailboats in Capri so we're looking forward to a wonderful vacation complete with swimming, dancing and sailing. We're going to Capri by plane. Doesn't it all sound exciting?

I had another very nice letter from John's folks. They seem like very fine people. John also had a letter from his folks saying they expected to hear from you sometime soon. If they don't hear they plan to write you first. I'd surely appreciate it, Mom, if you'd write them a letter. It's proper for you to write first. I know you aren't pleased about me getting married over here but Mom, if you can write to John and his parents I'd be awfully happy.

A Mrs. Goodwin from Haverhill wrote me the sweetest letter too. John said they're about the wealthiest people in town. Mrs. Goodwin said John was such a great friend of her son that she always considered him part of the family. She told me she's anxious for us to get back and she's already planning a reception to introduce me. John said every New Year's Day the Goodwins entertain 300 people in their home and it isn't even crowded!

We have a wonderful friend here in Mrs. Govoni. I told you about her. She's handling all the interpreting for the wedding preparations. She asked if she might enclose a letter to you, she said being a mother herself she knows how you must be worrying. I thought it was nice of her. When you answer this letter, perhaps you could enclose a letter for her? She is a wonderful friend and every one of us girls just loves her. She sort of mothers us all.

August 1944

Dear Mrs. Kriesel,

I think you have heard of me from LeOna. I feel that a few words from someone who knows both LeOna and John may ease your mind and make up for you not being present at the wedding.

I have known LeOna since she came here and I want to tell you right away that I think she is the sweetest girl I have ever met. You and Mr. Kriesel raised her well. As for John, he is just great in every sense of the word and you need never worry over LeOna's choice for her future. Your first glimpse at your new son-in-law will tell you that. I have a young daughter of my own and I understand what a mother may look for in a husband-to-be.

We will all be thinking of you on September 1st and I will try and give LeOna that little touch of motherly affection she will need that day. They are both so radiantly happy and we are all doing our best to help them through. I shall write to you again after the wedding to let you have a few impressions from our onlookers. I am quite sure my impressions will be lovely.

To you and Mr. Kriesel my very kindest regards and please don't worry one minute over LeOna and John, they are going to be a perfect couple.

Very sincerely yours,

Isaly Govoni

CUTTING A DEAL WITH POPE PIUS XII

LeOna often spoke about her Roman wedding and her most unusual interaction with Pope Pius XII.

Chaplain Stephen Cuff presided at my mother's memorial service in 2011. Father Cuff knew the story and in his eulogy he remarked, "I've loved knowing LeOna. Never before in my life have I known anyone, even people dressed in clerical robes as I am, who ever cut a deal with the Pope."

For anyone who knew LeOna it wasn't that much of a surprise.

LeOna tells her story as follows.

"September 1, 1944, I married Lieutenant John J. Cox in one of Rome's most beautiful basilicas, Saint Andrea Della Valle.

The lavish fresco decoration of the dome of Saint Andrea Della Valle represented one of the largest art commissions of its day. Two Italian Baroque painters of the Carracci school, Domenichino and Giovanni Lanfranco, completed the work in 1627. For many years the dome of Saint Andrea Della Valle was Rome's third largest, preceded by the Basilica of St. Peter and the Pantheon.

Ours was the first American wedding to be held in the basilica and it would be the first time a Catholic married a Protestant. As they put it, 'All Romans are Catholic.'

As it happened our wedding coincided with Pope Pius XII's address to the world. Because the Germans had blown up most of the Italian hydroelectric plants there was a real shortage of electricity. Our Red Cross liaison to the Vatican, who had been handling details of the wedding with church officials on our behalf, came to me shortly before the wedding and said I wouldn't be able to have electricity that day. He said Pope Pius XII planned to give an address to the world then and all available electricity would be requisitioned for his use only.

Now here I was planning this beautiful wedding. Music has always been such a large part of my life I couldn't imagine being married without it. One of the GIs had been a student at New York's Julliard School when he was drafted; he offered to play the large organ at the wedding. Another GI, who was an opera singer before the war, planned to sing the Ave Maria as I walked down the aisle. We had to have electricity or none of this would have been possible.

'Wait a minute,' I told our liaison, 'You tell the Pope it's the Red Cross girl from Minneapolis who's getting married. Tell him I know his speech to the world is important to him but my wedding is important to me as I only intend to get married once. Please tell the Pope that I'd really appreciate it if he'll share just one-half hour of his electricity, from 12:00 to 12:30 p.m. so we can have music. Tell him that if he does that I promise to raise all my children Catholic.'

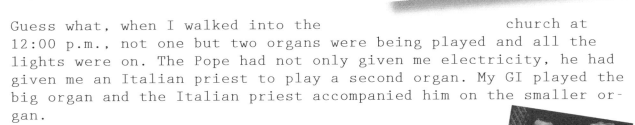

The liaison chuckled and said, 'I don't think so LeOna, this time you're definitely outranked.' However, I think just to humor me, he agreed to pass the message along to the Pope. Of course he never expected the message to actually get to the Pope but it did.

Guess what, when I walked into the church at 12:00 p.m., not one but two organs were being played and all the lights were on. The Pope had not only given me electricity, he had given me an Italian priest to play a second organ. My GI played the big organ and the Italian priest accompanied him on the smaller organ.

At exactly 12:30 p.m. the electricity went off."

"At exactly 12:30 p.m. the electricity went off."

Honeymooning on the
Isle of Carpri

Postcard images from Capri

September 1944

Dear Mom and Dad,

John and I just got home from a wonderful honeymoon. Before I go on I need to warn you about something, it's strictly against censorship regulations to have anything from our letters published in the newspaper. So please don't send anything about the wedding or our honeymoon to any newspapers.

We'll have pictures from the Army Pictorial Service and photographers from the 12th Air Force. I'll send them to you as soon as I get them but don't send any to the paper. Everyone told us our wedding was the nicest they'd ever attended. Especially with the beautiful music!

The church was beautifully decorated; the Italians even laid a red carpet down the aisle for us. Since ours was the first American wedding ever held in the cathedral they wanted to make it special. In the front there were live palm trees surrounded by ferns. The two altars had exquisite paintings by the artist Domenichino hanging over them. The top altar was covered with red velvet and had ornate, 3-foot silver candlesticks with huge, white candles. The lower altar was covered with white linen and lovely hand-made white lace. On either end of it were candelabras that held the seven candles of Jerusalem, which actually came from the Holy Land.

Thanks to Pope Pius XII, two organs were played. One was a huge pipe organ that stood in the cathedral; the other was a beautiful small organ that stood in the adjacent chapel. Golly, I was so thrilled with the music, everyone is still talking about it. After the organ recital one of our GIs sang the Ave Maria in Latin. It was so lovely that many people cried. As we left the church people showered us with rice, I think the Italians are still trying to figure out what that was all about!

The reception was lovely. In front of a beautifully set table was a huge basket of pink roses, a gift from the civilian workers in my club. On the table was a punch bowl made from the most beautiful glass I've ever seen and trays of artistically decorated small sandwiches. There were also huge glass bowls of chicken salad and trays covered with pastries of every description. The centerpiece was a big white heart covered with artificial orange blossoms. At the bottom of a heart was a scroll, tied on with a huge white satin bow. When we unrolled the scroll it was hand illustrated with caricatures representing our lives overseas, and a verse about how our families couldn't be here so the Red Cross workers wanted to be our families. They said the reception was their gift.

The American Red Cross organization gave us a suite of rooms at the Bernini hotel as a wedding gift. The suite had a bedroom, bath, kitchen and living room. Waiters dressed in tuxedos and tails served us dinner in the living room on a table decorated with pink blossoms. The only bad thing was the bed bugs. They are a real problem over here but we didn't expect to have them join us for our wedding night!

The next day we flew to Naples where we caught a boat for Capri. It was a two-hour boat trip and very lovely. As we arrived my friend Joanie Bunker met us with a jeep and trailer. She had arranged for a little orchestra to be at the boat but unfortunately the boat was two hours late.

We went to the Quisisana Hotel, the island's finest, where another of my friends, Jean Howard, had reserved the best room in the house for us. It had a big balcony overlooking the gardens and the Tyrrhenian Sea. Meals were served on a big outdoor patio where an orchestra played during lunch and dinner; it was just beautiful. The first morning I embarrassed John by eating two breakfasts. We had fluffy pancakes that reminded me so much of home my appetite increased by leaps and bounds.

We took a ride around the island in a horse-drawn carriage. Capri is built on a mountain so it's climb, climb, climb, wherever you want to go. The horse was all decorated with bells and plumes; the driver was almost as picturesque. He kept saying, "Me, I speak very nice English. I lived in 'Pilladelphie'."

160

Right: The wedding scroll

TO LEONA AND COXIE

We wanted to buy something to give the
                              bride and groom,
But when we looked in empty shops
Our hearts were filled with gloom.
So we put our heads together and
                    thought for over a week
And finally got a good idea, which we
                    think is most unique!

Since your families are too far away
To make a lot of fuss.
We want to be your family.
and have your wedding reception on
                              us!

Best wishes from
Ray Steeb
Mary Manson
Sally Steinman
Celia Senne
Fritzi Haugland
Esther Freeman
Dorothea Wilde
Virginia Watt
Verna Johnson
Howard Ross
Ruby McDonald
Eleanor Glenn
Eleanor Grannan
Mickie Frank
Ike Isemberg
Raeburn Rosendaal
Tony Rapolla
Liz Kehr

Rome 1st September 1944

John and I were impressed thinking we had an English-speaking driver. Gave him the address of some friends we wanted to visit in Capri but we never got there; despite the fact we rode around in his carriage all afternoon. That's when we realized he didn't speak English, 'Pilladelphie' was just one of a few words he knew.

The next day our fannies were so tired from bouncing along in that carriage we took a boat tour of the island. As we neared the famous Blue Grotto sea cave we had to transfer into small rowboats. The entrance to the Blue Grotto was through an opening just large enough for the rowboats; we had to lie flat on our backs and pull ourselves inside with a chain. Once inside the cave light from the

A postcard sent home from the honeymoon

entrance shined into the water and turned the green sea into the most beautiful blue color I've ever seen. I started to stand up to dive into that beautiful water and swim with all my clothes on. John grabbed hold of me and asked what the heck I thought I was doing.

The cobblestone walkways are something out of this world; they wind in and out all over the island. They were only wide enough for three to walk abreast, there are high walls on both sides. Ivy and flowering vines hung over the walls; it looked like a fairyland. We did lots of walking. John and I will never, never forget that beautiful place. We could have never had a wedding and honeymoon like that in the States. And to think it cost us $10 for the hotel and $5 (each) for meals.

My friend, Adelyn White, gave a dinner party for us at the villa where she lives on Capri. It once belonged to Princess Von Hess, the daughter of Italy's King Victor Emmanuel III, so it was actually a lavishly furnished castle. Our dinner table was decorated with clusters of purple flowers and seated 18 people.

Other friends took us to Gracie Field's villa where we were guests at a party given for Katharine Cornell and Brian Aherne.

In the 1930's Gracie Field was one of Britain's highest paid performers. She played to sold out theatres across the country. Katharine Cornell is known as the greatest American stage actress of the 20th century.

Brian Aherne was an Oscar-nominated stage and screen actor who was one of the top cinema character actors in the 1930s, '40s and '50s. He and Katherine Cornell were lifelong friends.

I'll wait until I get home to describe that villa. The fully furnished living room held not only the guests but an orchestra and a baby grand piano. And it wasn't even crowded! John and I got such a big kick out of meeting all the old "beat-up" baronesses, counts, princesses and artists at the party. John is still laughing about the world-famous artist we met, whose name we've already forgotten. John crosses his legs, poses his hand with his little finger straight out and says effeminately, "Oh, he was such a delightful man." The girls here just die laughing at his mimicking the nobility with his Irish humor. I think you'll get a kick out of John. He already knows he and Dad will hit it off after he read Dad's letter saying he was just glad I wasn't bringing home an Arab.

I hope you've written John's family by now. It's Mr. and Mrs. J.V. Cox, 17 Ferry St., Haverhill, Mass. They know the wedding took place because they wrote about it in a letter to John.

The phrase, "politically correct," was unheard of in 1944. Exposure to anyone or anything radically different was viewed as funny.

September 1944

Dear Mr. and Mrs. Kriesel,

As LeOna wrote to you today, I wanted to scribble off a few lines as well. We're both very happy and only regret that you couldn't be here to share in our happiness. Soon we shall all be together and we'll do it all over again.

Thanks to our friends we had a beautiful wedding, reception and honeymoon. Our pictures will be on their way soon. They show quite a bit of the affair. Many beautiful gifts were given to us and LeOna is going to send them to you for safekeeping.

My Mom and Dad are very anxious to meet my wife. They, and several of my friends, are ready to give her an "Eastern" reception. I know they'll be as proud of her as I am.

That is about all for now. My best to you and hope we all meet real soon.

Your son-in-law,

John

Postcard image from Rome

October 1944

Dear Mom and Dad,
The other evening one of John's friends from Haverhill, his name is Harry, had dinner with us. Before John came, Harry was telling me about John's family. Said he knew I'd like them as they are well liked by everyone. In fact, Harry's father owns the shoe factory where Mr. and Mrs. Cox had a lovely pair of shoes made for me.

Hello Mom Kriesel. LeOna is eating again. Yes, she's eating my rations.

John inserted that line while I dug in his rations for a candy bar. It seems I'm always hungry. You mentioned you thought I looked thin. Yes, I've lost considerable weight here in Italy as we're on what's known as combat rations. That's mostly rice, powdered eggs, canned meat, macaroni, canned fruit, peanut butter and grape jelly. Occasionally we get three tiny potatoes, each one a good mouthful. When we have string beans we get only one tablespoon. John's mother thinks he looks thin too.

LeOna & John Cox in St. Peter's Square after honeymoon

October 1944

Dear Mom and Dad,
I got a real nice letter from you yesterday. Yes, the wedding card came the day before the wedding. We were both very pleased with it, thank you. What kind of a letter did you get from Coxes? You didn't say.

Wednesday was our day off so John and I went to the opera, "The Force of Destiny," by Verdi. I don't know when anything has thrilled me as much as that did. The symphony orchestra itself was marvelous. The singers, the stage settings, the costuming—oh-h-h! Of course with Italy being the art center of the world and a leader in music, you can imagine what the scenery looked like. Really it was unbelievable! In one scene a stream flowed through two rocky mountain cliffs. The water was real and made little whirlpools as it flowed around the jagged rocks. I'm still wondering how that water flowed like it did.

The lighting effect made it look like evening with little stars that looked absolutely real. They use a revolving stage to set up all these elaborate scenes. It takes about five minutes between scenes. Anyway as I watched and listened to the music, I couldn't help thinking how old Professor Rust used to tell us stories about these beautiful pieces. Now here I am actually in one of the old countries, seeing it for myself. No wonder he had such a deep appreciation for music. It gives it an entirely different meaning when you see the story so beautifully recreated. I was so thrilled I'm going to try and see the whole series: Aida, Barber of Seville, Lucia de Lamaur (L'amour)and Il Travatore (Trovatore). Then I will hardly be able to wait until I get home and can practice my piano knowing the story connected with each piece of music.

Just think what a lucky girl I am. We want to go to the ballet. I've heard it's marvelous. John enjoys all this too, so we're making the most of every minute.

October 1944

Dear Mom and Dad,
Two of your letters, written a month apart, arrived the other day. John and I had a nice letter from Mrs. Goodwin in
Haverhill. She wrote that they (she and Mr. Goodwin) plan to
give us our silver as a wedding gift. She asked what pat-
tern I had chosen. Can you imagine anyone giving a gift like
that? I found pictures of silver and we're trying to choose.

I found a bunch of "costumes" stashed away behind a stage so
we had a big Halloween party. All of us Red Cross girls and
the civilian employees, dressed up in these terrible looking
costumes and had jack-o-lanterns made out of yellow squash
because, when we went to buy them, nobody could say "pump-
kin" in Italian. Everyone was all dressed up in costume.
We had a fortuneteller, fishpond, bobbing for apples, dart
throwing, a cake-eating contest, suitcase relay with girl's

clothes and a jitterbug contest. We even had a hog-calling contest.

I've taken over a new job and am I ever busy. I'm managing the whole club now and I'm concentrating on finding out what has been going on in the snack bar. I've already fired nine people. Four cashiers were coming out 400 to 1,000 lire short every night, that's when I discovered one of them was short-changing everyone. When the boys told me they had been short changed I confronted the cashier who insisted it wasn't true. She said the boys had been contributing money to the Red Cross and that's why they had less money in their pockets. I put some spies in the line and caught her; I couldn't catch the others so I just fired them on general principles. I know they were all stealing from us. We aren't having any more trouble now that we got rid of that group and hired a better class of worker. One of our new workers is an accountant and another recently graduated from medical school.

I also fired several old men who were supervisors in the snack bar. They never worked, only paraded around making themselves look busy. It seems they were teamed up with the black market and some awfully crooked deals are coming to light. They are mad at me and said they have reported me to the Communist organization. Honestly the stories I can tell you someday. Once you fire an Italian he hangs around the premises for several days giving you dirty looks and stirring up sympathy among the remaining employees. Today I got the military police and had one thrown out. Told him the next time I saw any of them around the place I'd have them all arrested.

When I went back to the club after we closed I walked into my darkened office and all the men I had fired, plus some other men, were sitting in a circle around my desk. They threatened that if I didn't hire them back there would be trouble; they indicated the men with them were Mafia. I was really scared but I didn't show it. I yelled at all of them to get out of my office that minute or I would get the Military Police. They left but they had made their point. Too bad, I won't be bringing them back, Mafia or no Mafia.

Another pose from the Halloween party

November 1944

Dear Karen,
'Tis a small world. Just met Mary Lou's roommate, Ginnie Good.
She's engaged to the most darling captain, he's really a honey.

Karen Karenin was a University of Minnesota roommate of LeOna's. Karen's husband Ed "Smokey" Keranen, was a member of the National Championship Gopher hockey team between 1938 – 1940. LeOna and Karen were often guests of Smokey Keranen at university hockey games. His teammate, All American John Mariucci, was part of their group.

John Mariucci, went on to become a formidable player in the National Hockey League and an outstanding coach. Mariucci was inducted into the United States Hockey League Hall of Fame and the NHL Hockey Hall of Fame. He also coached the silver medal United States Olympic Team. In his honor the University of Minnesota renamed the ice hockey facility the Mariucci Arena.

I have dysentery again; this is my tenth case! I've been in two
hospitals and now I'm in a huge general hospital and don't know
for how long. Such privacy, I'm "bed fourteen" in a rear hall just
outside the latrine. A wobbly screen with a sign "Women's ward"
separates us from hundreds of GIs sharing the hall. Think most of
the boys are about to be released. At least they sound perfectly
healthy with their guitars, accordions, harmonicas and the less
gifted giving forth on ocarinas. It's really an experience to be
in here.

Please greet Smokey for me and in the meantime don't forget how to
make french fries. I'm dying for some when I get home.

Love,
LeOna

Another snap from the Halloween party

November 1944

Dear Mom and Dad,
I'm sorry about not having written lots of letters recently but I have been so terribly busy. I've figured out new methods for supply control that are saving a lot of money. We're saving 44 pounds of sugar a day and that's just from the sugar we put out for coffee. We've saved 50% on costs for canned milk and I was able to reduce our sweet roll order by 2,000 buns a day. Now I am making an analysis of the ice cream plant to see what I can do with that. A lot of our supplies were being stolen so they could be sold on the black market.

Managing the club is interesting but it's hard work. These people take lots of supervision. If I spoke Italian it would be much simpler. Sometimes the workers make me so mad I could just scream; all I can do is LOOK at them. The other day a gas stove blew up and caught the awning on fire. The thing was going up in flames when an Italian boy came running into my office. My interpreter is Russian; she was a movie star before the war. I had to go through her to find out what was wrong; it took her so long to get the words out the place practically burned down. She said, "He ah em says…..the stofe….it ah ah is is is burning. There ah em ah is a fire."

I said, "OH for heavens sake," and grabbed the big fire extinguisher. It was too heavy for me to carry so I yelled at the boy to bring it. As we got out to the fire a little old man who is helping me control the supplies came running and yelled not to use the extinguisher because it cost duo-mille lire, which is about $20.00! That made me laugh so hard I will never forget it. Poor old fellow, at least he is one Italian civilian who's trying to save the Red Cross some money.

I've begun checking on the employees to see what they are doing and whether or not we needed their services. I saw that one woman is scheduled to arrive every morning at 6:30 a.m. I said, "What do you do at 6:30?" She said, "Scrub the porch."

Well last summer when we served outside it was probably necessary to scrub the porch every morning but certainly not now in the winter. So I asked her why she continued to do it? She gave me a blank look and said, "Because no one told me to stop." Then she said now it's so dark early in the morning she couldn't see what she was doing but she scrubbed anyway because that was her job.

Another old lady was coming at 6:30 every morning. When I asked what she did all I could get out of her was, "I clean the water closet." And apparently that's all she does but she's been doing it for years in this building so I just left her alone. My Dutch woman, Mrs. Koopman, is really good. She has feet the size of Myron Olson's and she's taller than John!

Myron Olson was a friend of LeOna's brother, Emmett. He had the biggest feet the two of them had ever seen.

Mrs. Koopman escaped from a Nazi concentration camp after two years of being imprisoned. She made her way to freedom by walking, riding on the backs of motorcycles and hiding in convents where the nuns protected her. Somehow she had managed to hide her jewelry from the Nazis. When she escaped she hid the jewelry in her shoes because she knew she could exchange jewels for money. When she finally got to the Netherlands she lived in The Hague.

I have two supervisors working under me, one is Russian, the other is Swiss. They both speak English very well and are dependable. A little Greek woman plays the phonograph; an English girl is a hostess. Now I hope to take on an American woman to make this a really international environment. Oh yes, my new interpreter is from Hungary.

You should see us all counting the cash every day. The bookkeeper counts out loud in Italian. Mrs. Koopman counts out loud in Dutch. I count out loud in English. When each of us finishes counting we write down how much money we counted so we can see if we all come out with the same amount. I would give anything if you could just walk in on me sometime, talk about a three-ring circus. Can't you just hear us? My hair is getting grey in front and I am not at all surprised.

December 1944

Dear Mom and Dad,
We have a Christmas tree in our snack bar that goes clear to the
ceiling. I had to make all the decorations which was quite a job
for such a big tree. John and I decorated a little tree in our
apartment last night, it's so cute. Andersons sent us a box of
presents; each one wrapped in Christmas paper so John hung them
on the tree. That made him curious as to whether you might have
wrapped our presents. John gets such a kick out of it when Christmas packages arrive I can hardly keep him from opening them. I said
I would look in his box so if things weren't wrapped he'd still
have a surprise on Christmas Eve. He said okay, he'd look in my box
to see if my presents were wrapped. As he looked inside my box he
said, "Oh—gee—lookit what's in here. It's just what you wanted. Oh
boy, you're going to like this." Then he wouldn't let me peek.

Honestly we've had more fun over these Christmas boxes than you
can imagine. Thank you very, very much. The only box John received
so far is the one from you; he was so tickled to get it yesterday.
We're having a nice time together and surely enjoy our two-room
apartment. He's so neat but sometimes it makes me nervous because
he's always organizing our things.

Hello Folks,

Thanks loads for the Christmas gifts. It was very thoughtful of you to think of me. Mrs. Kriesel, LeOna is awful to me. The wonderful soap you sent to me is now to be used by we. I guess I read the tag wrong.

Seriously, we're having a good time and I really do love my wife. Hope we both get home in the near future. I couldn't ask for a better wife. Take good care of yourselves, write often, and say hello to everyone.

Love,

John

December 1944

Dear Mom and Dad,
December 24th, we had a children's party in our snack bar. We planned for 150 kids and about 500 came. Things got off to kind of a bad start. There was a red suit in that old trunk with the Italian opera costumes I had found. We fixed it up and made it look like a Santa suit; one of the GIs volunteered to be Santa for the party.

Christmas card from Italy

What we didn't know was that Italians don't have Santa Claus like we do, they have an old witch called Befana who brings gifts to good boys and girls. When the children got to the party and saw Santa Claus, did they scream! We had told their parents to wait outside the club but when they heard their kids screaming and crying they started beating on the doors. We opened the doors just enough to tell them the kids were okay, said they were just frightened of the Santa costume. If we'd have opened the doors wider I'm sure the parents would have run in and grabbed them.

Fortunately, quick thinking Red Cross girls screamed, "Hand out the chawk-o-lots and ice cream!" Well, that worked. The kids calmed down and started eating ice cream and their parents stopped trying to beat the door down. The GIs were so tickled to share Christmas with children they stuffed them full of ice cream and cookies. One little Dutch refugee who spoke English said, "I et so much I'm sick."

Can you imagine seeing a big GI just in from the front playing woops-a-daisy with a little kid to make him stop crying? Another GI was feeding ice cream to a little tot and had the ice cream all over the kid's chin. Yet another was playing with three kids; he had one on each arm and the third one hanging onto his coattail. He was all in when it was over. The Italian ladies were all talking about how sweet the American soldiers are to children. The kids really took to the boys and loved them up so. Each GI had a kid riding on his shoulders. So in the end everything was good. Except for Santa who said, "I TOLD you it wouldn't work, dammit!" Oh well.

Christmas Eve, John and I attended midnight mass at St. Peter's in Rome. Did you hear the Christmas broadcast from St. Peter's? It was quite spectacular; the Sistine Chapel choir sang and silver trumpets were played. The Pope himself said mass. It was just fantastic; however the whole thing was ruined by the disorganized mobs of people in attendance. Several people were seriously injured. One

John clowning

American nurse had her leg broken. I'm sure I'd have been pushed right through the glass in a door if John hadn't given me one good shove that threw me clear. At one point I was pushed at such an angle my feet weren't on the floor; I was leaning at a 45° angle.

It seems the Polish army shoved one direction, the British shoved in another, the Italians in still another direction. Whenever an American was shoved he shoved back regardless of what direction. There were about 200,000 packed inside and equally as many outside trying to force their way in by smashing through the huge iron gates. I'll never get in a mob like that again, ever! John and I were glad to get home after that ordeal.

Christmas day was a big one at the club. We served about 10,000 in the snack bar. Had a big dance in the afternoon where I served cake and punch. We decorated the table with candles and poinsettias; the boys seemed to really enjoy everything.

John and I had a turkey dinner at the hotel after the party. We couldn't have asked for a better Christmas overseas. Hope we'll be home for the next one.

January 1945

Dear Mom & Dad,
Christmas was fun but I'm glad it's over. To get away for some rest
John and I took a trip to Sienna and Florence. We left on Thursday
and came back Sunday morning. As we drove north of Florence on the
highway to Bologna we heard the big guns firing away. One of the
towns we drove through must have been the site of quite a battle.
Talk about ruins! The way it smelled there must've still been people
under some of them.

In Sienna we stayed in an old castle. I slept in a sleeping bag;
which was certainly a new experience for me!

By mid-January 1945, Allied troops were just ten miles south of Bologna, however the city was not taken until the end of April 1945. The terrible conflict there was known as the Battle for the Gothic Line.

After finally breaking though the Gothic Line, Allied tanks overran the Po River valley. This battle marked the end of German organized resistance in Northern Italy.

February 1945

Dear Mom & Dad,
John and I have exciting news, we're expecting a baby! Remember I told you I hadn't been feeling very well? Now I know what was wrong with me. I'm feeling much better now and am awfully happy about that.

John's so excited about the baby he's like a big kid. He wanted to start thinking of names right away. I had to laugh at John already trying to name the baby because we only just found out there was going to be a baby! We're both really happy about it.

I'M COMING HOME SOON

February 1945

Dear Mom & Dad,
We're having the funniest winter weather here. At night it gets terribly windy and cold; it snows and hails at the same time so there's lightning and thunder in the snow! Italy is a funny place.

It looks like I'll soon be coming home. We've learned there's space available on a hospital ship that will be leaving shortly. Because I'm expecting a baby we think I'll get one of those spaces. Don't be worried; the ship will be well marked with a huge red cross so we should have a safe journey.

I'm so excited I can't stand it. I'm ready to come home and really ready to eat some of your good cooking Mom. I'm wondering, in the event you should be out of practice, would you mind trying a few chocolate pies, some home-made bread, cranberry relish, mashed potatoes with brown gravy and ask Annie to get her bean pot out? How I could go for some right now!

Gee-iminy I'm excited!

February 1945

Dear Mom & Dad,

I'm thinking so much about coming home I can hardly sleep any more.
Gosh it'll be so wonderful to see you. I'll probably eat you out of
house and home. I'm hungry for so many things. Decided to make a
list of what I want to eat so when I get there, if you ask me what
I'm hungry for and I'm too excited to think, you'll already know.

Here's what I want and boy do I want all of them!
Chocolate pie
Mashed real potatoes
Butter
Toast
Ham and eggs
Ginger bread
Cranberry relish
Dill pickles
Sauerkraut
A three-decker toasted sandwich
Baked beans
Fresh lettuce & tomato salad
Shrimp
Chocolate cake with fudge frosting
Escalloped corn
Dry cereal with fresh fruit
Fresh milk and any fresh fruit or vegetable

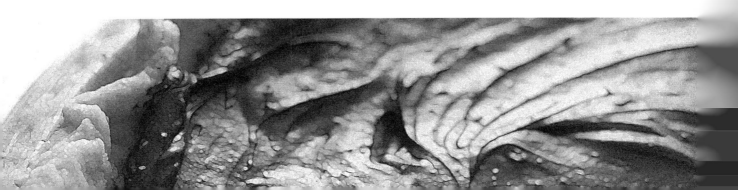

Things I never want to see again!
Dehydrated potatoes, carrots and apples
Grape jelly and orange marmalade
Preserved butter
Powdered egg omelets
Macaroni or spaghetti
Vienna sausage & spam
Canned fruit cocktail
Oatmeal
Canned milk

I think I'll be leaving within the week. You just can't imagine how happy I am to come home. John thinks he'll be home in a few months so we've agreed I should come to Ortonville to wait for him. That way if John isn't home in time for the baby's arrival I'll have you to help me. I'm going to need lots of help and I'm so excited to think about it!

When John does get home we'd like to stay with you for a while until we find out where John will work and where we can live. I hope that's okay.

The Red Cross ship Acadia, that brought LeOna home

March 1945

Dear Mom & Dad,
I found out today that I made it onto the ship; we'll be leaving tomorrow. They said it will take about 10 days to cross the ocean and we'll probably dock in Charleston, South Carolina. I'll come home from Charleston so look for me in a little more than two weeks!

I'll let you know when we arrive in Charleston. You won't be hearing from me until then.

See you real soon!

U. S. ARMY HOSPITAL SHIP
"ACADIA" ARRIVES
AT CHARLESTON, S. C.

POSTSCRIPT

Kathleen Nancy Cox with her father

November 2011

LeOna arrived home in March of 1945. I was born in August. My father made it to Ortonville the night of my birth; Dr. O'Donnell waited for him at the hospital, me in his arms.

Throughout her life my mother talked about her Red Cross experiences. She went on to resume her teaching career, became a best-selling author of educational materials, was inducted into Delta Kappa Gamma Society International, an honorary organization that recognizes outstanding female educators, and in 1983, she was elected to Who's Who of American Women. But it was in 1997, when she was included in the Women in Military Service for America Memorial at Arlington National Cemetery that gave her the greatest thrill.

It's fitting for LeOna to finish her own story. The following is taken from presentations she made to the American Red Cross Overseas Association, an organization she loved and whose members shared the same love for, and pride in, the American Red Cross. Here are the last of her tales.

One night when I was working at the Enlisted Men's Club the manager had to leave early. He asked me to go up to the third floor and answer the phone in his absence. As I approached the office our Yugoslavian medic, who manned the tiny first-aid station on the otherwise unoccupied third floor yelled, "LeOna, help! He's going to kill me!" With the medic pinned against a wall, a distraught soldier held an open knife to the medic's throat. "He's a no-good Eye-talian," said the soldier. "The Eye-talians killed my brother in North Africa and I'm going to kill him."

For a moment I froze. I couldn't yell for help because no one on the noisy floor below would hear me; I was going to have to handle this alone. The soldier was very young; as it turned out he'd been drafted between his junior and senior years in high school. He was obviously scared, homesick and out of his mind over losing his brother. I told him I had joined the war because my brother couldn't be drafted; I said I had come to help in his place. I said the medic he was trying to kill wasn't an Italian, he was Yugoslavian; his job was to save the lives of boys wounded in battle, like his brother.

Trying to remain calm and keep the conversation going I asked where the soldier was from. "Iowa," he said. "Well," I said, "I'm from southern Minnesota, not very far from Iowa." I stretched it a lit-

An official Red Cross poster produced by the U.S. Government during WWII

tle to make my hometown seem closer to Iowa. I said people from Iowa came to our lake to fish and hunt and that I loved Iowa people. "You can't beat midwestern people," I said, once again trying to establish a hometown bond.

After about 45 minutes of talking the medic and I were still alive and the GI seemed to have calmed down. "Let's go downstairs and have coffee and donuts and talk about Iowa and Minnesota," I ventured. The GI said, "You're going to turn me into the MPs." To which I responded, "Would you trust a girl from Iowa if she said she wasn't going to turn you in?" "Yeah," he said, "I would."

"Well I'm about as close to Iowa as you're going to get and besides, I run the snack bar," I explained. With that he took my hand and put the closed knife in it so I'd know he wasn't going to hurt me as we went down three flights of stairs in the dark.

"My name is LeOna," I said as we sat in the snack bar with coffee and donuts. "I'm Charlie," he said quietly. We continued talking about back home until it was time for him to go. I walked Charlie through a dark, wooded park to the army truck, his folded knife still in my hand. As he prepared to board the truck I said, "I'd like to shake your hand and wish you the very best until you're safely home with your family again." As we shook hands I slipped the knife into his and finished by saying, "I want you to have this because there may come a time when you need it. Be very careful how you use it so you don't do something you'll regret the rest of your life."

The next morning an MP came into the club and said, "Some guy turned himself in last night and said if it hadn't been for the Red Cross girl from Minnesota he would have killed a guy. The MP said, "Is that true?"

Red Cross girls with fresh doughnuts, offical U.S. Army image

The following Easter I was home in Minnesota when I received one of those Easter cards the GIs get. Inside the card it said, "Gratefully remembering your kindness, Charlie."

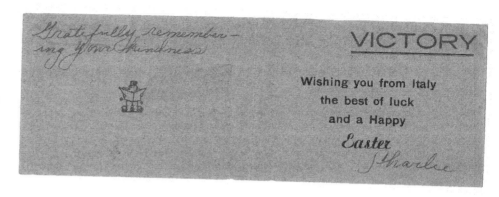

Charlie's Easter card

Several weeks later I had an experience of a different sort. This time I was playing the piano in our club. The boys, who all loved to sing, stood about four deep around the piano. All of a sudden one boy yelled, "Hey, you, playin' the pinnano, he says he knows ya. Let him tell how he knows ya."

I stopped playing and the boy in question said, "She's from my hometown. Growing up we didn't have any money and we wouldn't never have had Christmas presents if it wasn't for her and her brother. They always showed up at our house on Christmas Day with their father, and they shared their toys and candy with us."

Without looking I said, "Take off that army cap; if you have kinky blond hair you're a Kurtz boy!" He took off the cap and curls fell down around his face.

When I returned home I found out the Kurtz boy had been part of a unit that saw the most days in combat. The day after he was in my club his unit left Rome for Germany where the Kurtz boy stepped on a land mine and was killed. I couldn't stop crying. I will always feel the pain of not having had time to really talk to him that night. I was so busy playing the piano, trying to keep up the spirits of so many boys.

When I arrived back in the United States it was March 1945. I came on a hospital ship with a group of Red Cross girls and nurses. When we docked in Charleston Harbor we watched as wounded soldiers were carried from the ship on stretchers. We couldn't hold back our tears. A band was playing but it was not a joyous occasion. To get here we had sailed through storms and rough, rough seas for ten days. It was so rough waves washed right up through the portholes! Think how awful that had to be for those poor wounded soldiers.

People always ask what was the most exotic thing I saw in Africa, I tell them it was Arab men wearing burnooses, sitting in the sun, picking fleas from their clothes. They would lift their burnooses up and pull them around to the front in order to remove the fleas from the back. When they finished picking fleas and were getting up from the seated position, their burnooses would be wrapped around their waists which allowed their rear ends to stick out. What would they be wearing under those burnooses? Striped pants with big GI numbers on them! Turns out the GIs were trading their mattress covers to the Arabs. Because the Arabs couldn't get material they'd make pants out of the mattress covers.

When asked what I tired of most I'd say, "Answering, 'where yah from in the States,' a million times a day!"

The funniest? On Christmas Eve when I refused to wear my uniform and pulled out the beautiful black cocktail skirt and silver lame blouse I'd bought in Washington. I said to myself that no matter where I was in the world on Christmas Eve I was going to wear this outfit with my ankle-strap patent leather, high heels. I didn't care if I was shivering or not, it was fun. It was worth it to see how happy the GIs were to see an American girl dressed like an American girl on Christmas. Here's the funny part: before leaving Constantine for Rome, I sold that outfit. The woman who bought them had a questionable reputation around town. When she tried on my size 8 ½ shoes she exclaimed for all to hear, "Oh, grande!" She was exclaiming that my feet were big. All I could do was laugh.

THE STARS A

MEDITER

Vol. 2, No. 18, Saturday, April 8, 1944

Red Army Nears Total Liberation Of Ukraine Area

Soviets Battle Germans Eight Miles Outside Odessa Fortress

LONDON — Complete liberation of the slush-drenched south Ukraine appeared imminent at the week's end with Red Army heavy artillery battering the Black Sea fortress of Odessa while the battle-weary German 6th and 8th Armies reeled westward toward the Dniester River under unceasing Soviet pressure.

It was a race with death for German forces while German troops slogged westward through melting snows toward the crowded ferry terminal which is their only remaining escape route across the Dniester estuary into Rumania.

BBC reported Friday night that German "suicide units" had been

German Espionage Stalemated In U.S.

WASHINGTON — Crafty German military intelligence leaders have been stalemated in their persistent efforts to rebuild the spy rings which flourished in the United States before G-men smashed them early in the war, J. Edgar Hoover, Federal Bureau of Investigation chief, disclosed this week.

Mr. Hoover reported the Germans have been unable to establish a single successful spy although they have attempted to slip in operatives who posed as concentration camp refugees and, in one case, murdered an entire Jewish family to give a secret agent an excuse to enter the U.S. He did not elaborate on the incident.

Hollandia Lashed From Air

ALLIED SOUTH PACIFIC HEADQUARTERS — Strong relays of heavy Allied bombers swept over Hollandia, the strategic Japanese air base on the north New Guinea coast

Be

✚

The American National Red Cross
Overseas Service Certificate
to

Leona K. Cox

In recognition and appreciation of the faithful and meritorious performance of humanitarian service overseas in the Second World War as a representative of the American Red Cross

Franklin D. Roosevelt
PRESIDENT

Basil O'Connor
CHAIRMAN

ISSUED MARCH 31, 1945

American heavy bombers on
airfield at Zagreb, in north
Yugoslavia, yesterday.
MAAF's accomplishments
the week were far-reaching
appeared the
long time by
in Italy

Original document sent to 51st Troop Carrier Hdq. in Siena, Italy, 1945. Came by Cable.

```
LDLO V LDFI  NR-- UGENT   URGENT

T LDLO

FROM: M.A.T.A.F. Ø71610B

GR -BT-


THE CESSATION OF HOSTILITIES IN EUROPE HAS BEEN DECLARED

EFFECTIVE MAY SEVENTH PERIOD


BT - Ø71610B

GR-

SENT AT Ø7/1629B W.T.

ADVISE ALL SECTION

RCD NR --    AT Ø71637B  COH AR  K
```

Mary Jane Shelver was my neighbor in Ortonville, Mn. Her father was our doctor.

Telegram announcing the end of the hostilities in Europe

We Also Served Charter Member 268219

HIGHEST RANK: Not Applicable

SERVICE: Red Cross-O From Sep 1, 1943 to Jan 15, 1945

WAR / CONFLICTS: WWII Serving in: Algeria, Italy

BORN: Apr 5, 1915
BIRTH PLACE: Hudson, WI
MAIDEN: Kriesel
PREVIOUS:
NICKNAME:
SERVICE NAME:
DECORATIONS:

HOMETOWN: Oronville, MN

AKA:

MEMORABLE EXPERIENCES:

In 1944, in recently liberated Rome, enlisted men on R & R overflowed our American Red Cross Club. One night as I approached the office, our Yugoslavian medic who manned the tiny first-aid station on the otherwise unoccupied third floor yelled," Leona, Help! He's going to kill me." With the medic pinned against a wall, a distraught soldier held an open knife to the medic's throat. "He's a no-good 'Eye-talian'," said the soldier. "The 'Eyetalians' killed my brother in North Africa, and I'm going to kill him."

I dared not leave nor yell for help. Besides, no one on the noisy floor below would hear me. A half hour later, after I learned he was from Iowa, I told him that I was from southern Minnesota, calmly invited him to have a cup of coffee with me, and he trusted me. He gave me the knife, and through dark halls, we went down tothe basement kitchen. I was not afraid. Afterward, I took him to a truck that was leaving for camp, returned his knife, and he thanked me. Said an MP the next morning, "Some guy turned himself in last night and said, 'If it hadn't been for the Red Cross girl from Minnesota, I would've killed a guy.' Is that true?"

True. Although not a part of the military, as you see, our overseas' experiences were also many and varied.

REGISTERED BY:
HONORED BY: Fleming Rd United Church of Christ

LeOna Kriesel Cox's official entry in the Women's Memorial registry

Red Cross girls, they were something else.

Perhaps General Mark W. Clark, Commander of U.S. Forces in Italy during World War II, put it best when speaking at a Red Cross dedication in the White House Rose Garden.

The general said, "I well remember the story of a gravestone for a mule. It read, 'This mule, in its lifetime, kicked one colonel, 14 lieutenant colonels, 30 captains, 100 lieutenants, and one Red Cross girl.'" A sergeant seeing this epitaph summed up the prevailing sentiment when he said, 'That mule kicked once too often.'"

My mother died on February 24, 2011, just six weeks before her 96th birthday. The cause of death was dementia, a progressive disease from which she suffered the last 15 years of her life. She no longer recognized me and had lost the ability to communicate but almost to the end she could play the piano. She played from somewhere deep inside the brain where happy memories are stored. She always had a little smile on her face; I thought perhaps she was back in the Red Cross. Back in North Africa and Italy, with my dad, reliving the greatest years of her life.

I hope I was right.

LeOna and John Cox were married for 51 years
before John died.

Kathleen Cox is a storyteller, author and engaging public speaker. She is a graduate of The American University in Washington, D.C. School of Government and Public Service. Inspired by years of hearing her mother's World War II adventures, and having spent a summer studying in Europe, Kathie (as she is known) wanted to also spread her wings and do something adventurous. She became a Pan Am stewardess, based in Miami and New York and flew to Europe, South America and the Caribbean. Pan Am in the 1960's was glamorous, exciting and full of adventure.

Destination Unknown, Adventures of a WWII American Red Cross Girl, is Kathie's first book. Prior to writing it she has been a freelance writer, speaker, marketing consultant and creator/director of equestrian theatrical productions held in Madison Square Garden, Rockefeller Center, Belmont Park and venues throughout the United States and Europe.

Kathie's presentations from the book have been enthusiastically received by audiences of all ages. Comments have included the following: "I loved the drama and enthusiasm of the speaker," "Engaging personality, the letters are wonderful," and simply, "Great!"

To book Kathie for a speaking engagement or for further information, contact her at kathleencoxspeaks@gmail.com or online at kathleencoxspeaks.com.

Made in the USA
Charleston, SC
11 April 2012